Pro D3.js

Use D3.js to Create Maintainable, Modular, and Testable Charts

Marcos Iglesias

Apress®

Pro D3.js

Marcos Iglesias
San Francisco, CA, USA

ISBN-13 (pbk): 978-1-4842-5202-4
https://doi.org/10.1007/978-1-4842-5203-1

ISBN-13 (electronic): 978-1-4842-5203-1

Managing Director, Apress Media LLC: Welmoed Spahr
Acquisitions Editor: Louise Corrigan
Development Editor: James Markham
Coordinating Editor: Nancy Chen

Cover designed by eStudioCalamar

Cover image designed by Freepik (www.freepik.com)

Distributed to the book trade worldwide by Springer Science+Business Media New York, 233 Spring Street, 6th Floor, New York, NY 10013. Phone 1-800-SPRINGER, fax (201) 348-4505, e-mail orders-ny@springer-sbm.com, or visit www.springeronline.com. Apress Media, LLC is a California LLC and the sole member (owner) is Springer Science + Business Media Finance Inc (SSBM Finance Inc). SSBM Finance Inc is a **Delaware** corporation.

For information on translations, please e-mail rights@apress.com, or visit http://www.apress.com/rights-permissions.

Apress titles may be purchased in bulk for academic, corporate, or promotional use. eBook versions and licenses are also available for most titles. For more information, reference our Print and eBook Bulk Sales web page at http://www.apress.com/bulk-sales.

Any source code or other supplementary material referenced by the author in this book is available to readers on GitHub via the book's product page, located at www.apress.com/9781484252024. For more detailed information, please visit http://www.apress.com/source-code.

Printed on acid-free paper

To my mother, for discovering and nourishing my love for books.

Table of Contents

About the Author

Marcos Iglesias is a Senior Software Engineer who builds user interfaces at Eventbrite. He is passionate about creating test-driven data visualizations and dashboards using D3.js and front-end technologies such as ES2015, React, Redux, and Webpack. He enjoys writing about software, giving talks, and maintaining Britecharts, the open source charting library.

Marcos' experience releasing Britecharts and Britecharts-React gave him insights about creating, documenting, and publishing libraries as open source software. He has written blog posts for Smashing Magazine, Eventbrite's Engineering Blog, and Heart Internet. You can find him on Twitter @golodhros.

About the Technical Reviewer

Alexander Chinedu Nnakwue has a background in Mechanical Engineering from the University of Ibadan, Nigeria, and has been a front-end developer for over 3 years working on both web and mobile technologies. He also has experience as a technical author, writer, and reviewer. He enjoys programming for the Web, and occasionally, you can also find him playing soccer. He was born in Benin City and is currently based in Lagos, Nigeria.

Acknowledgments

I want to recognize Chris Viau for giving me the original idea and empowering me to write this book. His inspiration through his book *Developing a D3.js Edge* was vital. A lot of the material shown in *Pro D3.js* is a direct evolution of his work with the Reusable API pattern.

This book would not be possible without Mike Bostock, enabler and inspirer of the D3.js community. He not only gave us the tool (D3.js) but also showed us the path with his examples. Also, thanks to the D3.js community for their fantastic vibe and support to beginners and not-so beginners.

I am grateful to the software craftspeople: Kent Beck, Robert C. Martin, Martin Fowler, Michael Feathers, Steve Freeman, Ward Cunningham, Andrew Hunt, and Nicholas Zakas, among others. They taught several generations of developers on how to be proud professionals and care about our craft.

Last but not least, I want to thank Gloria Diaz, my partner, editor, and principal support. Thanks also to the Apress team and Alexander for their insightful reviews.

Introduction

Since its creation in 2011, D3.js has become the de facto standard for building complex data visualizations on the Web. D3.js development frequently starts by taking one of the community's many examples and using it as a way to jumpstart a new chart. This is a handy way to get something working fast so that you can iterate over it.

However, by working this way, you soon struggle to maintain, extend, or modify your visualizations. This problem is expected, as examples are made to demonstrate chart implementations and techniques, not to ship them to production.

How can you create data visualizations in a professional way?

This book walks you through the creation of maintainable, modular, and testable charts. It also helps you in packaging them into a library that you can distribute as open source software.

You will explore the process of creating a bar chart using D3.js and ES2015+ and encapsulating its code with the Reusable API pattern. You will also learn how to use and extend Britecharts, the reusable charting library based on this approach. You will discover how to write tests, document, and build your charts to create a charting library. Lastly, you will see how to use D3.js charts within React applications.

What's in This Book?

We have divided this book into 12 chapters. Here they are:

- **Introduction to Data Visualizations with D3.js**: Describes why D3.js and ES2015+ are the best options for creating data visualizations for the Web.

- **An Archetypal D3.js Chart**: Analyzes a typical D3.js chart example, walking through its code and reviewing the benefits and drawbacks of this approach.

- **D3.js Code Encapsulation and APIs**: Introduces different strategies developers use to encapsulate D3.js code, illustrating them with real-world library examples and advising how to pick one of them.

- **The Reusable API**: Presents this code pattern, which allows composable, extendable, configurable, and testable D3.js code encapsulation. It also discusses its advantages and drawbacks and how to overcome them.

- **Making the Bar Chart Production-Ready**: Walks through the steps necessary to take the initial archetypal example and transform it into a professional and reusable chart.

- **Britecharts**: Introduces Eventbrite's charting library, a set of charts and support components that follow the previous principles to help developers explore and interpret data.

- **Using and Customizing Britecharts**: Goes deep in the day-by-day use of Britecharts, showing how to compose the library components together to create compelling data visualizations.

- **Extending a Chart**: Extends the previous chapter by teaching how to extend Britecharts, modifying a chart and its documentation, and sending a pull request to contribute to the project.

- **Testing Your Charts**: Reviews on how to leverage the Reusable API pattern to test-drive a chart, using the initial bar chart as an example.

- **Building Your Library**: Illustrates how to build and publish an open source charting library using Webpack, Babel, and npm.

- **Creating Documentation**: Demonstrates the generation of documentation from source code comments, using GitHub Pages to host the docs and ESLint to enforce annotations.

- **Using Your Library with React**: Explores how to use D3.js within React.js applications, exploring different strategies and putting into practice one of them.

Code Examples

Alongside the text, *Pro D3.js* is supplemented with the source code for each code listing and example. You can find the code in this repository: `http://bit.ly/pro-d3-source-code`. Additionally, in some chapters, we mention extra code that we store in other repositories.

Who Should Read This Book?

We aimed this book for professional JavaScript developers that need to level up their D3.js code quality. Reading this book, you will focus on creating reusable chart components and packaging them into a library.

Pro D3.js will help you if you find yourself in one of these situations:

- You are a developer that knows the fundamentals of D3.js coding, and you have some experience creating and modifying D3.js charts. Now, you are wondering how to make your code more modular, extensible, and maintainable.

- You are an experienced front-end developer that wants to create tests for your charts. You need tests so that you can mercilessly refactor your D3.js code and add it to your continuous integration/deployment system.

- You are a developer that needs to maintain many charts with diverse quality and wants to figure out a way to not go crazy in the process.

- You are a senior developer or team lead that needs to allow different team members or even different teams to collaborate with the same D3.js codebase. Thus, you need a structured and error-safe way of coding chart components.

Pro D3.js discusses some of the fundamentals and usual patterns of D3.js code. However, we don't recommend this book for complete beginners to JavaScript and D3.js development.

CHAPTER 1

Introduction to Data Visualizations with D3.js

In this chapter, we introduce the field of data visualization. We will see why we need data visualizations and how we can use the Web to distribute them to achieve our communication goals.

We understand why D3.js is the de facto standard for data visualizations in the browser. We review the origins of the library, why it is so powerful and web focused. Also, we learn about the latest updates to the library.

Finally, we understand why ES2015 is the new standard for JavaScript. We review some of the new features and the benefits they bring, as well as how we leverage them when writing D3.js code.

Navigating a Data-Based World

We live in a world full of data. Big data has been a buzzword in the last years, and companies and governments are making use of data to influence their decisions.

Data visualization is about the creation and exploration of visual representations of data. With data visualizations – or dataviz – we communicate information clearly and efficiently. We do it by using charts, plots, and graphics.

We need to create data visualizations to help people interpret data "at a glance." When presented with a table of values, people need to "read" it before getting to any conclusion. On the other hand, data visualizations let users "see" the data right away, recognizing trends and comparing values.

The World Wide Web – or the Web – is everywhere. It is the most extensive information distribution channel ever created. JavaScript is also omnipresent. Browsers and servers run it, and you can find it in millions of devices. It is the most important programming language in the world.

© Marcos Iglesias 2019
M. Iglesias, *Pro D3.js*, https://doi.org/10.1007/978-1-4842-5203-1_1

When we need to create a data visualization to distribute to the whole world, we have many data visualization tools available. Which ones should we use? The answer is D3.js and ES2015. In the rest of this chapter, we discover why.

Why D3.js?

D3 stands for data-driven documents. It is a low-level JavaScript library that provides the building blocks to create interactive visualizations. The goal of D3.js is to enable web developers to build custom visualizations in the browser. All this with the smallest amount of effort and without giving up control over the final result.

Since its creation in 2011, D3.js (`https://d3js.org/`) has become the de facto standard for building complex data visualizations on the Web. In the next sections, we will see the benefits of this library and why you can't go wrong choosing D3.js.

Total Control of Your Visualizations

There are many ways in which we can represent data depending on the goal of the dataviz. A compelling data visualization can be

- A trend displayed in a line chart

- A comparison of values in a bar chart

- An event distribution in a heat map

- Percentages over the total in a pie chart

D3.js allows developers to create all of them – with no exceptions. The library grants you with almost limitless control over the look and behavior of your visualizations. For that, D3.js exposes a vast API (`http://bit.ly/pro-d3-api`) that includes, among other functions

- Mathematical functions to calculate complex drawings (d3-chord, d3-force, d3-hierarchy)

- Functions to operate over arrays of data and data structures (d3-array and d3-collection)

- Functions to select and transform DOM elements (d3-selection)

- Primitive functions to create SVG elements (d3-shape)

- Functions to map data into visual representations (d3-scale)

- Formatting functions to show dates and numbers (d3-time-format and d3-format)

- Functions to assign and manipulate colors (d3-scale-chromatic and d3-color)

D3.js is so thorough and complete that developers don't need any other support library to build complex dataviz.

Built for the Web

D3.js uses web standards like JavaScript, SVG, HTML5, Canvas, and CSS to assemble data visualizations that work in all browsers. One vital part of the Web is the ability to allow interactions and animations. These were key on D3.js creation, as we mention later, and in how it works.

In a nutshell, D3 loads data and attaches it to the DOM. Then it binds that data to new DOM elements and transforms those elements, transitioning among states if necessary.

D3 selections are at the core of the library. They allow to select DOM elements using CSS selectors and operate over them. We can change attributes and styles or add new nested elements inside the selected element. Listing 1-1 provides a quick example.

Listing 1-1. D3.js Selection

```
const svg = d3.select("body")
    .append("svg")
    .attr("width", 400)
    .attr("height", 200)
    .style("background-color", "purple");
```

In this code, we employed a selection to find the "body" tag in an HTML document. Then, we added a new SVG element with "append" and set the "width" and "height" attributes of it with "attr". Lastly, we styled the DOM element with a purple background color.

A D3.js selection (http://bit.ly/pro-d3-selections) is similar to the popular JavaScript library jQuery (https://jquery.com/). It helps us deal with SVG complexity

3

in a comparable way jQuery does with regular DOM elements. Both libraries share a similar chain-based API and the use of the DOM as data storage. Also, they shield developers from cross-browser compatibility issues.

Well Established

Mike Bostock got inspired by *The Grammar of Graphics* (`http://bit.ly/pro-d3-grammar-of-graphics`) (2005) to create D3.js. *The Grammar of Graphics* is a book by Leland Wilkinson that formalizes the building blocks of data visualizations. It establishes a system where the attributes of the dataviz (colors, shapes, and positions) map into the data. The relevance of Wilkinson's book is critical to understand the current data visualization tools.

Before D3.js, Bostock cocreated the data visualization toolkit Protovis (`http://mbostock.github.io/protovis/`). It was 2009, and he was in Stanford University gaining his PhD. Bostock released D3.js in 2011 (`http://vis.stanford.edu/papers/d3`), along with Vadim Ogievetsky and Jeffrey Heer. D3.js is a more expressive and performant evolution of Protovis. A crucial difference between them is that D3.js focuses on efficient transformations: animations, interactions, and state changes.

One of Bostock's decisions and a differentiating aspect of D3.js is the example-based learning. D3.js developers use example-aggregation sites to find more than 30,000 code examples. Sites such as `http://bl.ocksplorer.org/` and the fully featured `https://blockbuilder.org/search` make learning D3.js a lot easier.

Also, D3.js has a broad and supportive community, with a slack channel with more than 4000 registered users. There are many local meetups (`www.meetup.com/topics/d3-js/`) and a yearly unconference (`http://visfest.com/`).

Constantly Improved

Things in JavaScript land go fast, and no library can't stay still and keep its relevance. D3.js is no exception, and in the last years, it has been updated several times.

D3.js got a significant update in June 2016 with version 4.0. It became more modular, breaking the library into many submodules, and its namespaces got flattened. Version 4 got better canvas support, immutable selections, and shared transitions.

In January 2018, D3.js got updated to version 5. In this release, the core developers changed the data request APIs to use promises and removed some color scales. The update process was less extensive and problematic than with version 4.

Even with so many changes, Mike Bostock and the community updated the code examples to the latest versions. This avoided a split of the community, and most of the D3 developers are using today the newest versions of the library.

Why ES2015?

ES2015 is the denomination chosen for the new version of the JavaScript language for the browsers and node.js. Its name comes from the year where it became complete. ES2015 starts a new yearly release process, so the following versions are ES2016, ES2017, and so forth.

For the sake of simplicity, we only talk about ES2015, although we use some ES2016, ES2017, and ES2018 features in this book's code. In the next sections, we discover why we should use ES2015 to build our visualizations.

The New JavaScript Standard

ES2015 adoption has been complete. Nowadays, the leading web browsers support most of the new features (http://bit.ly/pro-d3-es2015-compatibility) except the modules. Also, surveys like The State of JavaScript (http://bit.ly/pro-d3-state-of-js) show that more than 85% of developers used ES2015 and would use it again.

The JavaScript compiler Babel (https://babeljs.io/) has been essential in the rapid adoption of ES2015 by developers. Babel also urged developers to use bundling tools like Webpack, of which we talk in Chapter 10.

Useful New Language Features

ES2015 adoption wouldn't have been so successful if it didn't introduce many practical features. In this book we use the following:

- Block-level declarations with let (http://bit.ly/pro-d3-mdn-let) and const (http://bit.ly/pro-d3-mdn-const)

- Template (String) literals (http://bit.ly/pro-d3-mdn-literals)

- Arrow functions (http://bit.ly/pro-d3-mdn-arrow-fn)

- Functions with default parameters (`http://bit.ly/pro-d3-mdn-default-params`)

- Rest parameters (`http://bit.ly/pro-d3-mdn-rest`) and the spread operator (`http://bit.ly/pro-d3-mdn-spread`)

- Object and array destructuring assignments (`http://bit.ly/pro-d3-mdn-destructuring`)

The specifics of these new features are out of the scope of this book. If you want to conduct a deep dive into them, I recommend Nicholas Zakas' book *Understanding ECMAScript 6* (`https://leanpub.com/understandinges6`). It is a thorough, sharp, and lucid book.

In this book's code, we use arrow functions widely. They make our code shorter and more to the point. We are also using parameter destructuring in functions, complementing them with default parameters.

Compact Code

ES2015 allows developers to reduce boilerplate code. Arrow functions, default function parameters, array and object destructuring, template literals, and the spread operator help us reduce code. Let's see some examples.

Destructuring

Destructuring and default function parameters make it easy to set variable or property defaults (Listing 1-2).

Listing 1-2. ES2015 destructuring and default parameters

```
// Before
function (object) {
    var radiant = object.radiant || ",
        luminous = object.luminous || ";

    // Use values
}
```

```
// With ES2015
function ({radiant = ", luminous = "}) {
    // Use values
}
```

The previous code demonstrates how tighter the extraction of variables can be. It could feel weird at first, but in my experience, you get used to it pretty fast. Also, the default values could be anything, even function calls!

Arrow Functions

Arrow functions are a new way of defining functions. They remove the "function" word and the need of binding the value of "this". These functions also allow implicit returns, making the code simpler (Listing 1-3).

Listing 1-3. Simpler code with ES2015 arrow functions

```
// Before
someArray.map(function(value) {
    return value + 1;
});

// With ES2015
someArray.map((value) => value + 1);
```

The use of arrow functions is very common these days. However, sometimes the "this" binding can be problematic when applied to some D3.js code. In most of regular JavaScript code, "this" either represents the current object or references a user interface event the user triggered. In D3.js though, "this" could also represent the current element in a D3.js selection. Proper variable naming and careful use of "this" are hence recommended to avoid this kind of issues.

Template Literals

Template literals make concatenating strings a thing of the past. Say "bye bye" to the "+" in your code. Check out Listing 1-4 to see an example.

Listing 1-4. String concatenation with ES2015 template literals

```
// Before
var newLight = "The new luminosity is " + light;

// With ES2015
let newLight = `The new luminosity is ${light}`;
```

Note how we use backticks (``` `` ```) instead of quotes and how we use the dollar symbol plus the curly braces to mark the interpolated variable.

Spread Operator

The spread operator, for objects and arrays, makes it easy to create, update, and combine these data structures. Let's see how in Listing 1-5.

Listing 1-5. Simple array and object combinations with the spread operator

```
// Before
var lightArray = [ 'radiant', 'vivid' ];
var newLightArray = lightArray.concat([ 'shiny' ]);

var baseLightObject = {
        a: 'radiant',
        b: 'vivid'
    };
var extraObject = { b: 'silvery' };
var merged = _.extend({}, baseLightObject, extraObject);
// using underscore.js or lodash
var merged = $.extend({}, baseLightObject, extraObject);
// using jquery

// With ES2015
let newLightArray = [ ...lightArray, 'shiny' ];

let merged = { ...baseLightObject, ...extraObject };
```

The JavaScript community uses this feature widely when creating immutable data structures. This practice helps reduce bugs produced by accidental state mutations.

Explicit Code

Some of the most celebrated features of ES2015 focus on making the code more explicit and overcome language quirks. Here are some examples of their use along D3.js.

const

"const" makes it easy to know how the developer employs a variable. It blocks the variable from being reassigned, such as in Listing 1-6.

Listing 1-6. No variable reassignments with const

```
const light = 'radiant';

light = 'silvery';
// Throws TypeError: Assignment to constant variable.
```

The JavaScript community has adopted a practice in which developers declare all variables as "const" at the beginning. We can change "const" to "let" if we need to reassign the variable.

Default Parameters and Destructuring

Default parameters help to distinguish if arguments are optional or required. Developers see it by looking at the function signature. Say goodbye to using the double pipe operator "||" in your code. See the example in Listing 1-2. Destructuring makes obvious what elements we expect within an object. See an example in Listing 1-7.

Listing 1-7. ES2015 destructuring on function signature

```
// Before
function (object) {
    var vivid = object.vivid,
        luminous = object.luminous;

    // Use values
}
```

```
// With ES2015
function ({vivid, luminous}) {
    // Use values
}
```

The difference is not huge, but if you add up the lines, it becomes significant.

Rest Parameters

Rest parameters make it easier to operate a variable number of parameters and remove the need for the "arguments" object (Listing 1-8).

Listing 1-8. ES2015 rest parameters avoid the use of arguments

```
// Before
function (a, b) {
    // Transform it into a real array
    var arrayOfArguments = [].slice.call(arguments);

    // Use arguments
}

// With ES2015
function (...args) {
    // Use args
}
```

Nowadays, you can avoid using the "arguments" object altogether. You won't need to do the transformation into a real array either!

Block-Level Declarations

Block-level declarations make us not rely on variable and function hoisting. This was confusing for newcomers to JavaScript, as shown in Listing 1-9.

Listing 1-9. ES2015 block-scoped variables

```
// Before
function wrapperFunction(light) {
    // The var declaration gets hoisted at this level

    if (light) {
        var newLight = light;

        return newLight;
    } else {
        // newLight here is 'undefined'

        return 'vivid';
    }
    // newLight here is 'undefined' too!
}

// With ES2015
function wrapperFunction(light) {
    // newLight doesn't exist here

    if (light) {
        let newLight = light;
        // or
        const newLight = light;

        return newLight;
    } else {
        // newLight doesn't exist here either

        return 'vivid';
    }
    // newLight doesn't exist here
}
```

No more of this disturbing behavior! Now a variable is available only within the curly brackets where developers define it. We are getting more errors, though, but that's good. Better to get the error when you are developing than in your production code.

Summary

In this chapter, you have learned why D3.js and ES2015 are the best options for creating data visualizations for the Web. We reviewed the characteristics that have launched D3.js to the zenith of data visualizations. We also saw why ES2015 got such a high adoption in a short time and which features we use along D3.js.

In the next chapter, we analyze a typical D3.js chart. We walk through its code and comment on the drawbacks of this kind of implementation.

CHAPTER 2

An Archetypal D3.js Chart

In this chapter, we'll learn about the example-based approach of learning and sharing D3.js code. We will review the canonical example that renders a bar chart. The code will serve as an illustration of what it is to work using a D3.js example as a jumpstart for your charts. We will learn about some of the standard code practices in the D3.js world and how they changed in the last versions.

Finally, we will analyze the example code critically, pointing out the drawbacks of its style and structure. We will see how it falls short when applying it to a professional software development context.

Examples in D3.js Development

Mike Bostock, the creator of D3.js, is a fan of examples. He gave a talk about examples in the Eyeo conference (`http://bit.ly/pro-d3-eyeo`) in 2013. He also created bl.ocks. org (`https://bl.ocks.org`), a site that allows developers to create, fork, and share D3.js code examples (or blocks). Bl.ocks.org inspired Ian Johnson to create Blockbuilder (`https://blockbuilder.org/`), which is an evolution with an improved example search and creation. The newest site for example sharing is Observable (`https://beta.observablehq.com/`). This site, cocreated by Bostock, provides developers with interactive code notebooks to build and share prototypes.

For Bostock, "examples are about demonstrating the potential value of ideas." For the D3.js community of developers, examples are also the primary way of learning D3.js:

- Examples show common code patterns and how to create complex visualizations.

- Examples explain new ways of doing things, inspiring developers to include them in their work.

© Marcos Iglesias 2019
M. Iglesias, *Pro D3.js*, https://doi.org/10.1007/978-1-4842-5203-1_2

- Examples expose what features do and, by giving real-world cases, why the features exist.

- Examples are great for sharing ideas in a lightweight and informal way.

To illustrate these benefits, we are going to review one of the canonical examples in D3.js development: a bar chart.

The Bar Chart Example

The "Let's Make a Bar Chart" tutorial article (`https://bost.ocks.org/mike/bar/`) by Mike Bostock is one of the most popular D3.js tutorials for beginners. In this three-part tutorial, Bostock goes over the process of creating a D3.js bar chart. You can find the final code in the "ch2/original-bar-chart.html" file of the book repository. Let's now examine the implementation. It all starts with adding an SVG element to the HTML and downloading D3.js, as shown in Listing 2-1.

Listing 2-1. Bar chart example HTML file

```
<svg width="960" height="500"></svg>
<script src="https://d3js.org/d3.v4.min.js"></script>
<script>
    // Chart code here
</script>
```

See how we are using version 4 of D3.js, as this was the latest version shared in a block. Bear with me, later we'll update it to version 5. The SVG element acts as a container for the rest of the SVG markup. It also establishes a different coordinate system, in which the origin is situated in the top left corner of the SVG container. In Listing 2-2, we store a selection of the root SVG element in a variable and create a margin object.

Listing 2-2. Bar chart root SVG and margins

```
var svg = d3.select("svg"),
    margin = {top: 20, right: 20, bottom: 30, left: 40},
    width = +svg.attr("width") - margin.left - margin.right,
    height = +svg.attr("height") - margin.top - margin.bottom;
```

Note how we use the "+" unary operator to transform the width and height properties of the root container from strings into numbers. This allows us to subtract the margins and figure out the internal chart dimensions that we save in the "width" and "height" variables.

In the two lines of code in Listing 2-3, we are creating "x" and "y" variables that store the scale functions.

Listing 2-3. Bar chart scales

```
var x = d3.scaleBand().rangeRound([0, width]).padding(0.1),
    y = d3.scaleLinear().rangeRound([height, 0]);
```

Scales are the functions that "glue" the dimensions of our chart together with the data that we want to present. Scales need to have both a range of pixels and a domain of data. In this case, we are only setting the ranges and the padding of the scales, as we need the data to fix their domains.

The Margin Convention

In the next code snippet, we are selecting the SVG root element and creating a "g" element (http://bit.ly/pro-d3-mdn-g) that works as a container for other SVG elements. For that, we are using the Margin Convention (http://bit.ly/pro-d3-margin-convention) to control the positioning of the chart. You can see it in Listing 2-4.

Listing 2-4. Bar chart margin convention setup

```
var g = svg.append("g")
    .attr("transform", "translate(" + margin.left + "," + margin.top + ")");
```

The Margin Convention is a useful pattern that helps us avoid headaches when moving our SVG elements around. Once this pattern is arranged, the rest of the chart code can ignore margins altogether.

Loading Data

Next, we are fetching the data using one of the D3.js request helpers. Then we apply a cleaning function that coerces the value to a number by using the unary operator "+" again. In Listing 2-5 you can find an example.

Listing 2-5. Bar chart data loading (version 4)

```
d3.tsv("data.tsv", function(d) {
  d.frequency = +d.frequency;

  return d;
}, function(error, data) {
  if (error) throw error;

  // Rest of code here
});
```

There is a caveat here though, as this code won't be valid in version 5 of D3.js. All the data request code has changed in the last version of D3.js, moving into a promise-based API using the "d3-fetch" (http://bit.ly/pro-d3-fetch) module. The new implementation looks like the code in Listing 2-6.

Listing 2-6. Bar chart data loading (version 5)

```
d3.tsv("data.tsv")
    .then((data) => {
        return data.map((d) => {
            d.frequency = +d.frequency;

            return d;
        });
    })
    .then((data) => {
        // Rest of code here
    })
    .catch((error) => {
        throw error;
    });
```

Notice how we need to create a data-cleaning function and apply it once we receive the data. Another difference is that we are not checking for errors in our callback, but listening for them in the "catch" clause of the promise chain. I have created a fork of the bar chart example (`http://bit.ly/pro-d3-bar-chart-v5`) in blockbuilder.org, so that you can see a working example updated to D3.js v5.

Scales and Axes

Once we have loaded the data, we can finish configuring our scales with their domain. The domain is the range of data that the chart covers. Check Listing 2-7 to see how we specify it.

Listing 2-7. Bar chart scale domain setting

```
x.domain(data.map(function(d) { return d.letter; }));
y.domain([0, d3.max(data, function(d) { return d.frequency; })]);
```

The "x" scale includes the whole set of letters. The "y" scale goes from zero to the largest frequency value from all the letters. Now that we have our scales ready, we can draw both axes by appending "g" elements and labels, as we do in Listing 2-8.

Listing 2-8. Bar chart axes drawing

```
g.append("g")
    .attr("class", "axis axis--x")
    .attr("transform", "translate(0," + height + ")")
    .call(d3.axisBottom(x));

g.append("g")
    .attr("class", "axis axis--y")
    .call(d3.axisLeft(y).ticks(10, "%"))
      .append("text")
        .attr("transform", "rotate(-90)")
        .attr("y", 6)
        .attr("dy", "0.71em")
        .attr("text-anchor", "end")
        .text("Frequency");
```

In these two blocks of code, we have drawn both horizontal and vertical axes. To do it, first we created "g" elements and added classes to them. Then, we have called the axes functions (d3.axisLeft and d3.axisBottom) on the "g" elements. We also added a rotated text to the y-axis, labeling it as "Frequency."

Drawing Bars

Previously, we have created the SVG container and the scale functions. Then, we drew the axes, and finally, we are going to draw the bars – the main point of the chart. In Listing 2-9, we use SVG rectangles or "rect" elements.

Listing 2-9. Bar chart bar drawing

```
g.selectAll(".bar")
    .data(data)
    .enter().append("rect")
      .attr("class", "bar")
      .attr("x", function(d) { return x(d.letter); })
      .attr("y", function(d) { return y(d.frequency); })
      .attr("width", x.bandwidth())
      .attr("height", function(d) { return height - y(d.frequency); });
```

In the previous code, we can see how Mike Bostock used the enter/update/exit pattern to create a new SVG rectangle for each datum in the data set. In a nutshell, we are repeating all the instructions that come after "enter()" call for each data entry.

In this book, we are not going to dig deeper into the details of the enter/update/exit pattern. If you want to learn more about it, this block (http://bit.ly/pro-d3-eue-pattern) gives a demonstration. You read the Thinking with Joins blog post (https://bost.ocks.org/mike/join/) to better understand the logic behind this pattern.

Output

In the end, we have a block that looks like the code in Listing 2-10.

Listing 2-10. Complete bar chart example code

```
<!DOCTYPE html>
<meta charset="utf-8">
<header>
    <style>

    .bar {
      fill: steelblue;
    }

    .bar:hover {
      fill: brown;
    }

    .axis--x path {
      display: none;
    }

    </style>
</header>
<body>
    <svg width="960" height="500"></svg>
    <script src="https://d3js.org/d3.v5.min.js"></script>
    <script>

    var svg = d3.select("svg"),
        margin = {top: 20, right: 20, bottom: 30, left: 40},
        width = +svg.attr("width") - margin.left - margin.right,
        height = +svg.attr("height") - margin.top - margin.bottom;

    var x = d3.scaleBand().rangeRound([0, width]).padding(0.1),
        y = d3.scaleLinear().rangeRound([height, 0]);
```

```
var g = svg.append("g")
    .attr("transform", "translate(" + margin.left + "," +
    margin.top + ")");

d3.tsv("data.tsv")
    .then(function(data) {
        return data.map(function(d) {
            d.frequency = +d.frequency;
            return d;
        });
    })
    .then(function(data) {
        x.domain(data.map(function(d) { return d.letter; }));
        y.domain([0, d3.max(data, function(d) { return d.frequency;
        })]);

        g.append("g")
            .attr("class", "axis axis--x")
            .attr("transform", "translate(0," + height + ")")
            .call(d3.axisBottom(x));

        g.append("g")
            .attr("class", "axis axis--y")
            .call(d3.axisLeft(y).ticks(10, "%"))
          .append("text")
            .attr("transform", "rotate(-90)")
            .attr("y", 6)
            .attr("dy", "0.71em")
            .attr("text-anchor", "end")
            .text("Frequency");

        g.selectAll(".bar")
          .data(data)
          .enter().append("rect")
           .attr("class", "bar")
           .attr("x", function(d) { return x(d.letter); })
           .attr("y", function(d) { return y(d.frequency); })
```

```
            .attr("width", x.bandwidth())
            .attr("height", function(d) { return height - y(d.frequency); });
    })
    .catch(function(error) {
        throw error;
    });

</script>
</body>
```

This renders a bar chart like that shown in Figure 2-1.

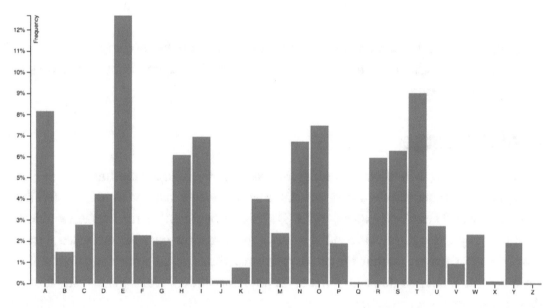

Figure 2-1. *Rendered bar chart*

We have a bar chart that works, right? It works, and you could copy this code, change it a bit, and use it somewhere on your web site. Nevertheless, we cannot consider this codebase an example of professional, good-quality, and production-ready code. Let's see why.

Problems with D3.js Example Code

In this section, we are going to point out some of the problems with the code in Listing 2-10. The following drawbacks are common to every block you can find in bl.ocks.org or blockbuilder.org.

Hard to Read

Anybody not used to D3.js won't find this code understandable. First, because this implementation is a monolithic function. To know what this code is doing, developers need to read from top to bottom. Moreover, this code deals with many concerns all at once. If we choose to extend its functionality, this file's length could get out of hand quickly.

Another reason this code is not readable is due to the number of chained declarations. Code chaining produces compact code that is concise, but too much of it is difficult to understand.

Hard to Change

The code in Listing 2-10 is hard to modify. Say we want to change something, for example, the number of ticks on the y-axis. We would need to change a hardcoded value in line 55: ".call(d3.axisLeft(y).ticks(**10**, "%"))". This is not ideal. A better implementation would start by extracting all hardcoded values and strings into constant variables at the top of the file. Once we do that, we could try to make those parameters configurable. However, this is not possible with the current implementation. We need an abstraction that allows configuring the chart.

Not Reusable

If we needed several instances of this chart, how would we go about it? We would need to duplicate the code that many times. Duplication increases maintainability costs and coupling. It also creates room for bugs and overlooked or forgotten code. These are all issues of code repetition, and we want to avoid them.

Not Composable

Usually, data visualizations include several elements such as legends and tooltips. With the current implementation, if we have extra functionality, we would need to copy and paste their code too. Again, not ideal. To be able to create rich visualizations effectively, we should compose the chart code with other pieces.

Fragile

The current code is very brittle: we won't know if it keeps working once we change any line of code. Also, we won't be able to refactor it either. This is especially challenging when working with a demanding library as D3.js, where most of the times our initial solution won't be the best one.

The software development solution to this problem is testing. The code in Listing 2-10 is not tested, and as it is now, it would be tough to test. This prevents us from using a technique that ensures a lower level of bugs and higher code quality: Test-Driven Development (TDD). Again, we need a proper code structure that allows us to test our chart code.

Summary

In this chapter, we have learned about the particular relation of D3.js development and example code. We reviewed the canonical example of a D3.js chart. We walked through some common patterns of D3.js code and discovered why they are necessary.

We learned why examples are great for sharing ideas in a lightweight and informal way. However, we also saw how using an example code to build a production D3.js chart is a bad idea.

In the next chapters, we will discover a more professional way of building D3.js charts. It is a way that overcomes all the drawbacks mentioned in this chapter. Before doing so, we will see how different libraries have solved the structuring problem of D3.js code.

CHAPTER 3

D3.js Code Encapsulation and APIs

In this chapter, we will review the different ways we can abstract D3.js code. We realize how the different encapsulations map to different API flavors. We will examine examples of those APIs in production-ready D3.js libraries, how do they look in the real world and their results.

Finally, we discuss the aspects to take into consideration when choosing the best API for your project and context.

Encapsulation in D3.js Code

As we discovered in the previous chapter, we need an abstraction to encapsulate our D3.js code. This abstraction should solve the problems we highlighted in the example code, namely: lack of clarity, configuration, reusability, composition, and testability.

Since its rise to popularity in 2012, D3.js developers have come up with multiple ways of abstracting their code. Their background and preferences have influenced them, and up to now, there is no clear winner.

Because there are so many coding flavors and levels of abstraction, we can get confused about which way to go when choosing the API of our chart library. As it is usual in the software world, the right choice depends on the context. At the end of this chapter, we examine how you can get closer to the best solution.

© Marcos Iglesias 2019
M. Iglesias, *Pro D3.js*, https://doi.org/10.1007/978-1-4842-5203-1_3

API Flavors

The D3 community hasn't found a standard way of creating components from D3.js code. This is a frequent need as D3.js is remarkably low level. We could say that there are as many encapsulation patterns as D3-based libraries. We are going to classify them into four groups: Object Oriented, Declarative, Functional, and Chained or D3-like.

Object Oriented

Object-Oriented Programming or OOP is one of the most popular programming paradigms. When developers code in OOP, they organize code within objects. These are data structures that group the data and the methods used to operate in that data. In practice, OOP in JavaScript looks a bit like Listing 3-1.

Listing 3-1. Object-Oriented Programming example

```
let chart = new Chart({ type: 'Bar', color: 'blue', data: [...]});
chart.render();
```

In the previous example, we created an instance or a chart by calling "new" in the Chart class. After that, we called the "render" method on that chart instance to draw the visualization.

Declarative

Declarative Programming is one of the two main approaches to programming, along with Imperative Programming. The former focuses on telling our code "what to do," in contrast with the latter, which developers use to specify "how to do it." In our context, a declarative API would look like the code in Listing 3-2.

Listing 3-2. Declarative Programming example

```
let chart = Chart.create({
    type: 'Bar',
    container: '.container',
    bar: {
        color: 'blue',
```

```
        padding: 5
    },
    data: [...]
});
```

See how the amount of code is minimal in this example, it is mostly configuration.

Functional

Functional Programming (FP) is a programming paradigm that understands programs as a series of mathematical functions applied to data. FP code avoids keeping global state, makes this state immutable, and favors the use of "pure functions."

A pure function is one that returns the same output given the same input. Pure functions don't have side effects and avoid using the global state. Due to this, pure functions are reusable and predictable. Developers can create complex operations by composing pure functions. In Listing 3-3, we see a hypothetical example of a functional style in our context.

Listing 3-3. Functional Programming Example

```
let dimensions = {width: '400', height: '300'};
let xAxis = Library.categoricalDataAxis(x, dimensions, data);
let yAxis = Library.numericalDataAxis(y, dimensions, data);
let representation = Library.bars(dimensions, data);

let chart = Library.compose(xAxis, yAxis, representation);
```

In this code, we are creating components for axes and bars. Later, we use a compose function to bring all together to create a chart.

Chained

A Chained API is one that uses method chaining as its syntax. Method chaining is a common way of invoking many method calls within Object-Oriented languages. The idea is that every time the developer calls a method, the code returns the original object. This way, developers can keep on calling methods of that object in the same statement. A benefit is that they won't need to create variables to store the results of each function call.

The Smalltalk language, an Object-Oriented dynamically typed language created in the 1970s, originated this syntax. D3.js itself works in this way. Let's see an example extracted from the "d3-selection" documentation (Listing 3-4).

Listing 3-4. Chained example

```
d3.selectAll('p')
    .attr('class', 'graf')
    .style('color', 'red');

// equivalent to
var p = d3.selectAll('p');
p.attr('class', 'graf');
p.style('color', 'red');
```

Note how this Chained API (also named "Fluent Interface") allows for a more concise code. We are saving two statements and the creation of one variable.

Example Libraries

I have researched D3.js libraries to gain an overview of the ecosystem. You can see the results of the research in this spreadsheet (`http://bit.ly/pro-d3-research`). I have picked a limited set of libraries that represent the API styles described in the previous section.

The selected projects use one of the latest D3.js versions. They also feature high-quality code, broad test coverage, or innovative approaches. They differ in the granularity of their abstractions (high, medium, or low level) and the style of their API.

For the following comparison, we use the data set employed in the chart of the previous chapter, as shown in Listing 3-5.

Listing 3-5. Letter frequency data set

```
export const letterFrequency = [
    {
        "letter": "A",
        "frequency": 0.08167
    },
    {
        "letter": "B",
        "frequency": 0.01492
    },
```

```
//...
    {
        "letter": "Z",
        "frequency": 0.00074
    }
];
```

Note how we use a simple named export to make this data array available to the charts.

Plottable

Plottable (`http://plottablejs.org`) is a popular Object-Oriented Programming charting library (Figure 3-1). The team at Palantir Technologies created and maintained the library since 2014.

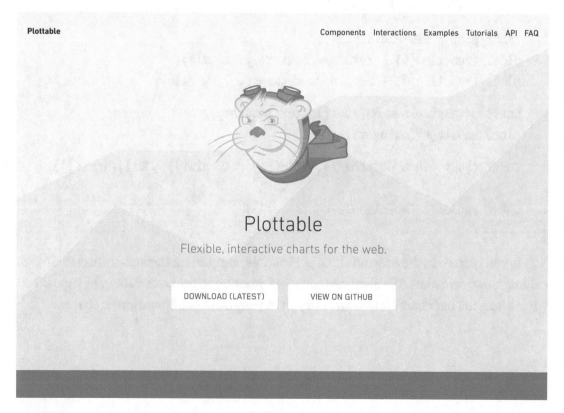

Figure 3-1. Plottable homepage

Plottable is a set of low granularity components that developers can use to compose data visualizations. When using this library, we need to set up axes, scales, and plots manually to create a chart. Let's see how our archetypal bar chart looks in code with Plottable (Listing 3-6).

Listing 3-6. Bar chart with Plottable

```
import {letterFrequency} from './dataset';
import {Scales, Axes, Plots, Dataset, Components} from 'plottable';

require('plottable/plottable.css');

export const plottableBarChart = function() {
    const xScale = new Scales.Category();
    const yScale = new Scales.Linear();

    const xAxis = new Axes.Category(xScale, "bottom");
    const yAxis = new Axes.Numeric(yScale, "left");

    const plot = new Plots.Bar();
    plot.x(function(d) { return d.letter; }, xScale);
    plot.y(function(d) { return d.frequency; }, yScale);

    const dataset = new Dataset(letterFrequency);
    plot.addDataset(dataset);

    const chart = new Components.Table([[yAxis, plot], [null, xAxis]]);

    chart.renderTo("#plottable-container");
}
```

As you can see in the previous listing, Plottable component instances are created by calling "new" on a class. We also pass some information to the constructor. In Figure 3-2 we see how the bar chart looks without applying any extra configuration or styling.

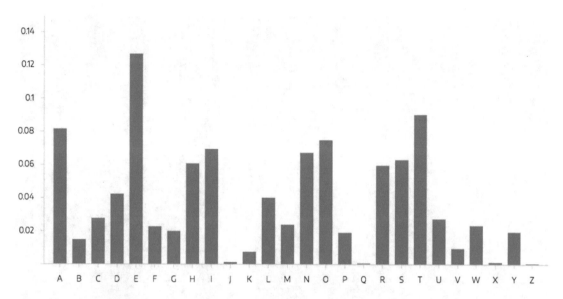

Figure 3-2. *Rendered bar chart with Plottable*

Plottable is a library formed by a set of modules, classes, interfaces, and types. These denominations serve as proof of the OOP influence on the creators of this library.

Billboard

Billboard (`https://naver.github.io/billboard.js/`) (Figure 3-3) is a fork of the classic C3.js (`http://c3js.org/`) library updated with D3.js version 5. This library pretends to give continuity to the abandoned C3.js project.

Figure 3-3. *Billboard homepage*

Billboard.js is written using ES6, ES modules and a modern build process including Babel and Webpack. The API of Billboard is high level and based on configuration objects passed to chart generation functions. We could group Billboard among the declarative API libraries, and we can see an example of it in Listing 3-7.

Listing 3-7. Bar chart with Billboard

```
import {letterFrequency} from './dataset';
import {bb} from 'billboard.js';

require('billboard.js/dist/billboard.css');

export const billboardBarChart = function() {

    // Data formatting
    const categories = letterFrequency.map(({letter}) => letter);
    const frequencies = letterFrequency.map(({frequency}) => frequency);
```

```
bb.generate({
    data: {
        x: "x",
        columns: [
            ["x", ...categories],
            ["frequency", ...frequencies]
        ],
        type: "bar"
    },
    axis: {
        x: {
            type: "category"
        }
    },
    bindto: "#billboard-container"
});
}
```

As you can see in the preceding code, developers don't need to specify axes; Billboard renders them by default and adds a tooltip, as shown in Figure 3-4.

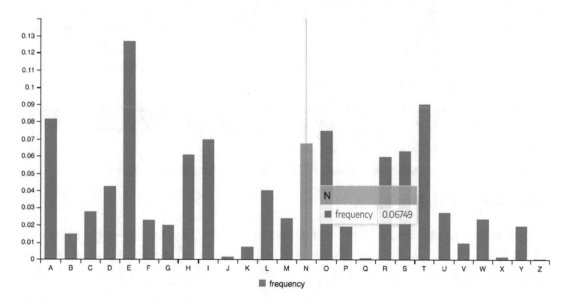

Figure 3-4. *Rendered bar chart with Billboard*

Billboard is excellent news for developers that had old code in C3.js, as they can port it to an up-to-date library like Billboard without hassles.

Vega

A project that takes the declarative path a bit further is Vega (`https://vega.github.io`). It evolves the configurations from JavaScript objects into pure JSON files. Vega (Figure 3-5) implements a visualization grammar inspired by *The Grammar of Graphics*, the book that was an inspiration for D3.js.

Figure 3-5. *Vega homepage*

You can play around with Vega in its editor (`http://bit.ly/pro-d3-vega-editor`), selecting one of their examples as a starting point. Let's see in Listing 3-8 how our bar chart configuration looks like in Vega.

Listing 3-8. Bar chart specification in Vega

```
{
  "$schema": "https://vega.github.io/schema/vega/v4.json",
  "width": 800,
  "height": 400,
  "padding": 10,

  "data": [
    {
      "name": "table",
      "values": [
        {"letter": "A", "frequency": 0.08167 },
        {"letter": "B", "frequency": 0.01492 },
        {"letter": "C", "frequency": 0.02782 },
        {"letter": "D", "frequency": 0.04253 },
        {"letter": "E", "frequency": 0.12702 },
        {"letter": "F", "frequency": 0.02288 },
        {"letter": "G", "frequency": 0.02015 },
        {"letter": "H", "frequency": 0.06094 },
        {"letter": "I", "frequency": 0.06966 },
        {"letter": "J", "frequency": 0.00153 },
        {"letter": "K", "frequency": 0.00772 },
        {"letter": "L", "frequency": 0.04025 },
        {"letter": "M", "frequency": 0.02406 },
        {"letter": "N", "frequency": 0.06749 },
        {"letter": "O", "frequency": 0.07507 },
        {"letter": "P", "frequency": 0.01929 },
        {"letter": "Q", "frequency": 0.00095 },
        {"letter": "R", "frequency": 0.05987 },
        {"letter": "S", "frequency": 0.06327 },
        {"letter": "T", "frequency": 0.09056 },
        {"letter": "U", "frequency": 0.02758 },
        {"letter": "V", "frequency": 0.00978 },
        {"letter": "W", "frequency": 0.0236 },
```

```
        {"letter": "X", "frequency": 0.0015 },
        {"letter": "Y", "frequency": 0.01974 },
        {"letter": "Z", "frequency": 0.00074 }
      ]
    }
  ],

  "signals": [
    {
      "name": "tooltip",
      "value": {},
      "on": [
        {"events": "rect:mouseover", "update": "datum"},
        {"events": "rect:mouseout",  "update": "{}"}
      ]
    }
  ],

  "scales": [
    {
      "name": "xscale",
      "type": "band",
      "domain": {"data": "table", "field": "letter"},
      "range": "width",
      "padding": 0.1,
      "round": true
    },
    {
      "name": "yscale",
      "domain": {"data": "table", "field": "frequency"},
      "nice": true,
      "range": "height"
    }
  ],
```

```
"axes": [
  { "orient": "bottom", "scale": "xscale" },
  { "orient": "left", "scale": "yscale" }
],

"marks": [
  {
    "type": "rect",
    "from": {"data":"table"},
    "encode": {
      "enter": {
        "x": {"scale": "xscale", "field": "letter"},
        "width": {"scale": "xscale", "band": 1},
        "y": {"scale": "yscale", "field": "frequency"},
        "y2": {"scale": "yscale", "value": 0}
      },
      "update": {
        "fill": {"value": "steelblue"}
      },
      "hover": {
        "fill": {"value": "red"}
      }
    }
  },
  {
    "type": "text",
    "encode": {
      "enter": {
        "align": {"value": "center"},
        "baseline": {"value": "bottom"},
        "fill": {"value": "#333"}
      },
      "update": {
        "x": {"scale": "xscale", "signal": "tooltip.letter", "band": 0.5},
        "y": {"scale": "yscale", "signal": "tooltip.frequency",
        "offset": -2},
```

```
        "text": {"signal": "tooltip.frequency"},
        "fillOpacity": [
          {"test": "datum === tooltip", "value": 0},
          {"value": 1}
        ]
      }
    }
  }
 ]
}
```

We load this JSON configuration with Vega's view API, as shown in Listing 3-9.

Listing 3-9. Bar chart loading in Vega

```
import {loader, parse, View} from 'vega';

export const vegaBarChart = function() {
    let view;

    loader()
        .load('src/charts/vega.json')
        .then(function(data) { render(JSON.parse(data)); });

    function render(spec) {
        view = new View(parse(spec))
            .renderer('svg')  // set renderer (canvas or svg)
            .initialize('#vega-container') // initialize view within parent
            DOM container
            .hover()              // enable hover encode set processing
            .run();
    }
}
```

Using together the loader and JSON configuration, we get to render the chart as we now see in Figure 3-6.

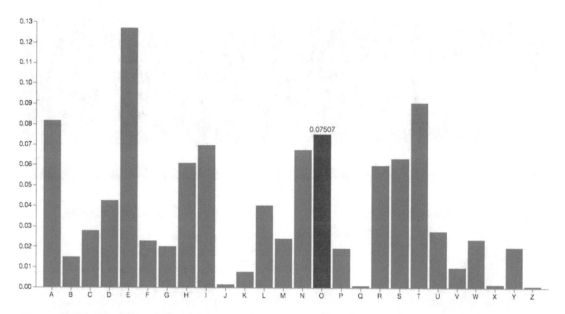

Figure 3-6. *Rendered bar chart with Vega*

The Interactive Data Lab of the University of Washington created Vega. Maybe that's why this library is so fashionable among academic circles. Vega is usually a great choice when looking for a quick and style-agnostic conventional chart.

D3FC

D3FC (`https://d3fc.io/`) is a functional, low granularity library. D3FC (Figure 3-7) makes use of D3.js and functional components to help us create powerful interactive charts both in SVG and Canvas.

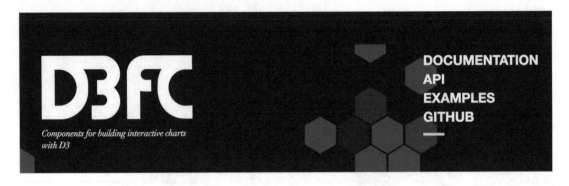

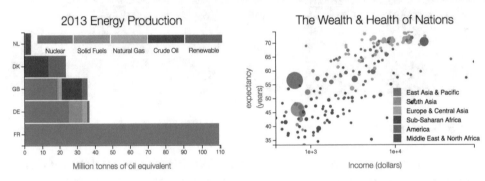

Figure 3-7. *D3FC homepage*

This is a thought-provoking project, especially with the intensive use of D3.js when developing with it. Although powerful, D3FC has a steep learning curve. You can check out their examples (`http://bit.ly/pro-d3-d3fc-examples`) to see what you will be able to do with the library. In Listing 3-10 is the code for our bar chart.

Listing 3-10. Bar chart with D3FC

```
import {letterFrequency} from './dataset';
import * as fc from 'd3fc';
import * as d3 from 'd3';

export const d3fcBarChart = function() {
    const barSeries = fc.autoBandwidth(fc.seriesSvgBar())
        .crossValue(d => d.letter)
            .align('left')
```

```
    .mainValue(d => d.frequency)
    .decorate((selection) => {
        selection.select('path')
            .style('fill', 'steelblue');
    });

const yExtent = fc.extentLinear()
    .accessors([d => d.frequency])
    .pad([0, 0.1])
    .include([0]);

const chart = fc.chartSvgCartesian(
        d3.scaleBand(),
        d3.scaleLinear()
    )
    .xDomain(letterFrequency.map(d => d.letter))
    .xPadding(0.2)
    .yDomain(yExtent(letterFrequency))
    .yTicks(10, '%')
    .yOrient('left')
    .plotArea(barSeries);

d3.select('#d3fc-container')
    .datum(letterFrequency)
    .call(chart);
}
```

Note how the code in the previous listing doesn't differ much from regular D3.js code. The most innovative part of D3FC is the ".decorate" method. It allows developers to access the internal elements just before rendering them. Observe the result of our bar chart in Figure 3-8.

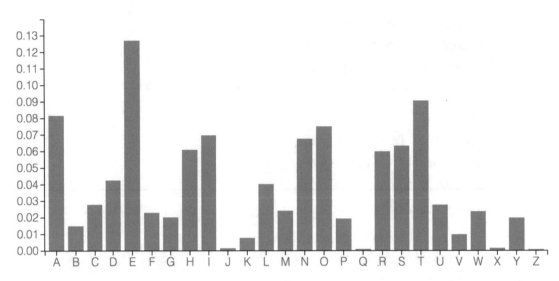

Figure 3-8. *Rendered bar chart with D3FC*

D3FC adds a thin layer of abstraction over D3.js, making it easy to do ordinary tasks. All that while keeping the option to modify the internal d3 selections. That's why I think D3FC is an attractive choice for D3.js power users.

Britecharts

Britecharts (http://eventbrite.github.io/britecharts/) is the charting library we created at Eventbrite. We based Britecharts' interface in the Reusable Chart API, a pattern we analyze in detail in Chapter 5. See in Figure 3-9 a screenshot of Britecharts' homepage.

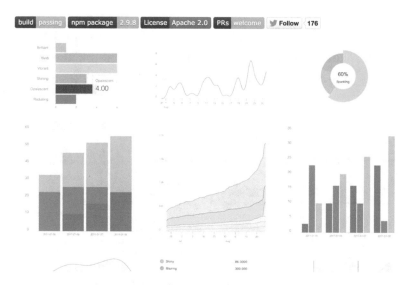

Figure 3-9. Britecharts homepage

Britecharts employs a mid-to-high-level encapsulation, making it easy to create charts. It keeps a low complexity on the inside, allowing D3.js developers to use the library as the origin of their own "forks." Let's see how we use the library in Listing 3-11.

Listing 3-11. Bar chart with Britecharts

```
import {letterFrequency} from './dataset';
import {bar} from 'britecharts';
import {select} from 'd3-selection';

require('britecharts/dist/css/britecharts.css');

export const britechartsBarChart = function() {
    const barChart = bar();
    const barContainer = select('#britecharts-container');
```

```
barChart
    .valueLabel('frequency')
    .nameLabel('letter')
    .width(800)
    .height(400);

barContainer.datum(letterFrequency).call(barChart);
}
```

In the previous code, we see how Britecharts uses a D3.js selection as a container for the chart. We have previously attached data to the container using "datum," the data needed to build the chart. This code outputs what we see in Figure 3-10.

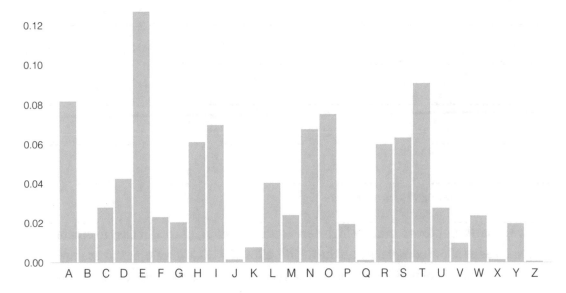

Figure 3-10. *Rendered bar chart with Britecharts*

We spent much time polishing the user interface of Britecharts. We also added demos (http://bit.ly/pro-d3-britecharts-demo) and created complete documentation to make it easy to get started with it.

Comparing Their APIs

We have discussed four different code paradigms and some D3.js-based libraries that exemplify them. In the diagram in Figure 3-11, we can see a summary of these libraries grouped by their APIs.

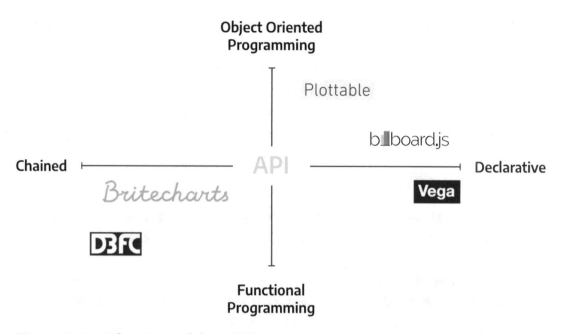

Figure 3-11. *Libraries and their APIs*

The previous chart gives you a high-level overview and is biased to my limited experience with these libraries. I have created a demo repository (`http://bit.ly/pro-d3-library-demo-repo`) with these five bar charts, and you can see them in action in the demo page (`http://bit.ly/pro-d3-library-demo`). The intention is to allow you to play with the results and dive into the code.

Choosing an API for Your Library

In previous sections, we learned about different API flavors. We also saw various D3.js libraries' APIs and how they look like in practice. However, when we choose the best API for our library, we must evaluate our context and the specific goals of the library that we want to prioritize. Let's discuss some of the considerations in this section.

Developers Background

The background of the developers that create and use the library is critical when deciding for an API. Either you work on the library by yourself or with a team, you should ask yourself which paradigms you are more used to. Do you come from an OOP or FP world? Are you experienced D3.js developers or do you look for a solution that involves as little code as possible?

If we look at your team and background, we could say that D3.js and JavaScript developers would like something closer to the Chained or FP styles. However, developers with a traditional OOP background like Java or C++ would feel more comfortable with OOP or declarative APIs. Non-tech savvy users prefer the declarative approach.

Library Objectives

We need to think about the goals of our library to figure out the level of abstraction we want to manipulate. High- and low-level abstractions offer different levels of flexibility and expressiveness.

High-level abstractions are easy to use because developers need to learn one or two modules. This means that they get exposed to less API surface. However, high-level libraries limit the combinations to create complex visualizations. The customization options are also restricted. If you want to prioritize ease of use against flexibility, choose a high level of abstraction.

In opposition, low-level abstractions are harder to learn and use. Low granularity components imply extra modules, so developers need to check the APIs of more elements to compose them. Yet, low-level encapsulations enable almost limitless combinations of charts and vast personalization options. Note that remarkably low-level libraries compete against D3.js itself, so their abstractions must be relevant to justify the investment.

Summary

In this chapter, we learned the most common ways of encapsulating D3.js code. We also saw real-world examples of libraries that embody those strategies. Finally, we discussed some considerations when picking an API.

Probably at this point, you already have a favorite style. In the next chapters of this book, we dive deep into the Reusable Chart API and Britecharts. Don't feel distressed if that was not your preference, most of the principles we'll discuss over apply to any API.

CHAPTER 4

The Reusable API

In this chapter, you will learn the Reusable API, the abstraction that we use in the rest of this book. We will discover how we can use this pattern to craft reusable modules, and we will review its benefits and how to use it.

Lastly, we learn how to work around its drawbacks, and grasp the Reusable API seamless combination with D3.js.

Background

As we saw in Chapter 2, the archetypal bar chart, the example-based approach is not enough to create professional D3.js charts. We need an abstraction to wrap our D3.js code and solve the problems we mentioned:

- Readability

- Hard modification

- Reusability

- No composability

- Fragility

In Chapter 3, we reviewed some of the different types of encapsulation and the APIs they generate. There are many more. In this book, we are going to learn the Reusable API. We chose it because it is easy to create and use, it has lots of benefits, few drawbacks, and the D3.js community loves it. In the rest of this chapter, we go deep into these reasons, so keep reading.

© Marcos Iglesias 2019
M. Iglesias, *Pro D3.js*, https://doi.org/10.1007/978-1-4842-5203-1_4

Ease of Use and Creation

We all want to use libraries that are easy to use. As creators of quality charts, we also want to work with code that is readable. We want all this without sacrificing our development experience or increasing the complexity of our code.

The Reusable API is a pattern to create modules that provides privacy and an interface based on getters and setters. It also allows us to group the creation of the charts' main building blocks. We do this by calling functions within the core of the pattern, as we see in the next section.

The Pattern

As a disclaimer, this version of the pattern and the following code evolved from the implementation in *Developing a D3.js Edge* and *Mastering D3.js*. These two great books were vital for the development of the Reusable API as we show it here.

We'll use the code in Listing 4-1 as the core of the pattern.

Listing 4-1. Reusable Chart API core pattern

```
import * as d3 from 'd3';

function chart() {
    // Private Attributes declaration

    function exports(_selection) {

        _selection.each(function(_data) {
            chartWidth = width - margin.left - margin.right;
            chartHeight = height - margin.top - margin.bottom;
            data = _data;

            buildScales();
            buildAxis();
            buildSVG(this);
            // .. Rest of building blocks

        });
    }
```

```
    // API

    return exports;
};

export default chart;
```

This ES2015 module exports a function called chart. Calling this function returns another function that accepts a D3.js selection as input. The code in Listing 4-1 loops over the elements contained in the selection. This "each" allows us to create several charts with different data. For each of those container elements, it extracts the data from the DOM to build a chart, using the same element as a container.

Thanks to this process, we can create several charts with the same configuration and different data. To configure these charts, we need to support a way of modifying the internal variables. We do this by using getters and setters, as shown in Listing 4-2.

Listing 4-2. Reusable Chart API accessors

```
exports.height = function(_x) {
    if (!arguments.length) {
        return height;
    }
    height = _x;

    return this;
};
```

The previous code attaches to the exportable module a function named height. We call these functions "accessors," and they accept either one parameter or zero. When we pass a value to the accessor, we set that value as the height parameter. However, if we don't pass any value, then we use this function to return the current value of the height parameter. By writing this code, we are creating a getter and a setter within the same function.

Note how we can perform operations on the value before setting it. We could check the value with a validator, so we make sure the value is a number; we could also set the width, if we had a fixed aspect ratio set in the chart. Let's see an example in Listing 4-3 of the margin accessor we use in Britecharts.

Listing 4-3. Margin accessor

```
exports.margin = function(_x) {
    if (!arguments.length) {
        return margin;
    }
    margin = {
        ...margin,
        ..._x
    };

    return this;
};
```

See how, in this case, we are not setting the provided value right away. We are creating a new object using the spread operator. We first spread the current values of the margin (top, bottom, left, and right), using them as default values to the new object. Then, we spread the provided values for the margin, overriding the default ones. This way, we allow users to provide as many key-value combinations of the margin object as they desire, using the current values as defaults.

Using the Reusable API

In the previous chapter, we saw an example of the use of Britecharts. Using the Reusable API in practice looks more or less the same. See Listing 4-4 for an example.

Listing 4-4. Using the Reusable Chart API

```
import * as d3 from 'd3';
import chart from 'chart';

const data = [...];
const myChart = chart();
const container = d3.select('.container');

myChart
    .height(300)
    .width(600)
    .margin({
```

```
        top: 20,
        bottom: 20,
    });
```

```
container.datum(data).call(myChart);
```

The previous code creates an instance of a chart and uses a D3.js selection to wrap the DOM element with the class "container". Then, we configure the chart using the height, width, and margin accessors. In the last step, we add the chart data to the container element by using the "datum" method, and we call the chart on the container.

We can also create different instances of the same chart. Listing 4-5 shows us how.

Listing 4-5. Creating multiple charts with the Reusable Chart API

```
import * as d3 from 'd3';
import chart from 'chart';

const myChart = chart();

const data = [...];
const container = d3.select('.container');

const alternativeData = [...];
const alternativeContainer = d3.select('.container-alt');

myChart
    .height(300)
    .width(600)
    .margin({
        top: 20,
        bottom: 20,
    });

container.datum(data).call(myChart);
alternativeContainer.datum(alternativeData).call(myChart);
```

Notice how in this listing we only needed a second data set and an extra container. This code renders two similar charts that live together on the same page without conflict.

Ample Benefits

In Chapter 2, we learned about the issues we experience when using example code directly in our systems. They were many. Let's now review them and see how the Reusable API addresses the problems.

Simplicity

D3.js charts tend to grow a lot, especially when different stakeholders push for including their favorite features on a chart that was going to be "a simple thing." The good news is that it's easy to change Reusable API components. We only need to think beforehand which parameters we want to make configurable and add API accessors for them. Besides, if we don't expect them to be configurable and the requirements change, it's a matter of minutes to make parameters available.

Working within a team on D3.js charts can be an absolute pain if everybody uses an example-based approach. With the Reusable API though, teamwork is more convenient. D3.js has a pretty steep learning curve, so modularizing the parts of a chart into small pieces helps junior members of our team. They will be able to jump into the code and own it.

This approach also fosters collaboration and communication. Every team member can work on different components of the visualization. Because every chart has a given API that we can agree upon beforehand, we avoid complications while working.

The Reusable API adds structure to our D3.js charts. It involves writing more code. However, it is a predictable code, as most of the building blocks are present in all charts. Using named functions to build the blocks of the charts allows us to explain what that code is doing, as well as reuse the functions between charts.

This structural predictability empowers developers to adjust and refactor their charts. We see an example in Chapter 5 of a refactor from the example code into a Reusable API module.

Modularity

The main reason the Reusable API pattern can improve our D3.js chart code is modularization. It won't be a surprise for engineers: splitting large problems into smaller ones has been a fundamental problem-solving technique since the earliest days of science. With the Reusable API, we can separate the different parts of a large and complicated chart into several components.

Another advantage is that we can bundle all these components into a package. We can create our own charting library and distribute it as an NPM module. We discover how to build and publish modules in Chapter 11.

Reusability

We already saw how we could create multiple instances of the Reusable API charts. Moreover, this pattern makes it easy to reuse the code we write. Reusability won't apply to all of our code, but most of the small components that form a data visualization (think tooltips, brushes, legends) can be completely reusable.

For the main chart component, whether it is a bar, line, area, or pie chart, we can use its structure and building blocks to create similar charts. For example, if we have a bar chart and want to create a line chart from it, we can probably reuse the functions that create the x- and y-axes, the tooltips, and the legend.

Composability

The Reusable API pattern allows us to compose large data visualizations from small components. We could do this in two different ways:

- **Accepting components as configuration**: This approach allows using other components inside the charts. We could pass in components with different configurations depending on our specific needs for the parent component.

- **Hooking components to each other by using event handlers**: We can create instances of the charts first and then make them communicate through events. This strategy implies that most components expose event handler functions in their APIs.

Through the use of a shared methodology of creating components, we can compose them intuitively. We see specific examples of creating large systems from small pieces of functionality in Chapter 8.

Testability

My favorite reason for adopting the Reusable API is that it allows us to test our charts. We can build small units of functionality with a given interface that we can test most of the times. These components do one thing and do it right. The increased focus reduces the number of dependencies, which is one of the main challenges when testing. You won't even need mocks!

D3.js is hard, and charts can become complicated. Being able to refactor our initial implementations is a critical part of keeping our code clean. Clean and DRY (`http://bit.ly/pro-d3-DRY`) code unlocks faster development, fewer bugs, and higher flexibility. These are qualities of professional D3.js code.

Moreover, being able to test our charts means that there won't be problems getting their code into our continuous integration tool. This combination allows us to catch bugs before they reach production.

Few Drawbacks

We have seen what composes a Reusable API chart and how to use it. We learned how it solves the problems we mentioned in Chapter 2. However, as in most software solutions, choosing a strategy comes with tradeoffs.

In this section, we read about the short list of drawbacks mentioned by developers when using the Reusable API and how to overcome them.

Increased Complexity

Making our charts reusable forces us to increase the complexity of the chart code. Reviewing Listing 4-1, we could claim that the loop over the different containers is something we didn't need before. Also, we require first to create instances of our components before using them.

There isn't an escape from this. It is part of the tradeoff between the ease of use and the power of the abstraction. It is the same tradeoff between high and low granularity abstractions we talked about in Chapter 3. The good news is that we can always tweak it. In this book, we empower you to take the code and change it as you seem fit when writing your charting library.

Inefficient Property Updates

One drawback of the Reusable API that developers mentioned is the need for re-calling the charts when updating some value. Let's take the typical example of updating the width of a chart to fit variable screen sizes. See how we do it with the Reusable API in Listing 4-6.

Listing 4-6. Updating properties

```
import * as d3 from 'd3';
import _ from 'underscore';

import chart from 'chart';

const data = [...];
const myChart = chart();
const container = d3.select('.container');

myChart
    .height(300)
    .width(600)
    .margin({
        top: 20,
        bottom: 20,
    });

container.datum(data).call(myChart);

const redrawChart = function(){
    const containerWidth = container.node()
        .getBoundingClientRect()
        .width;

    myChart.width(containerWidth);

    container.call(myChart);
};
```

```
// Redraw chart on window resize
const waitTime = 200;
window.addEventListener(
    'resize',
    _.throttle(redrawChart, waitTime)
);
```

Observe how we need to call our chart for every width change. We would need a similar implementation when updating other properties of the chart, including the data.

A proposed way of avoiding re-calling the chart would be to include an "updateWidth" accessor and call it when the width changes. You can see more details of this approach in the following article (http://bit.ly/pro-d3-update-functions). Implementing "update functions" for all the chart properties won't be scalable, but if your specific case requires it, you could add some of them.

As a side note, see how in the previous code we throttled the call to "redrawChart". This precaution is necessary because the resize event triggers several times in a short time lapse. In this case, we have chosen 200 milliseconds as wait time between successive calls to "redrawChart".

Boilerplate Code

Creating an extensive library of charts using the Reusable API could incur in a large amount of boilerplate code. This code includes the accessor functions, the logic for sizing the chart, labeling, and event handling.

For the accessor code, there is a way of limiting the repetition. The solution is to generate the code of the accessors. In Listing 4-7 we see how it would look like for simple getters/setters.

Listing 4-7. Accessor generation

```
import * as d3 from 'd3';

function chart() {
    // Private Attributes declaration
    const privateAttribute1 = 'value';
    const privateAttribute2 = 'value2';
    //...
```

```
// Public Attributes declaration
const publicAttributes = {
    margin: {
        top: 10,
        right: 10,
        bottom: 10,
        left: 10,
    },
    width: 960,
    height: 500,
};

function exports(_selection) {

    _selection.each(function(_data) {
        //...

        buildScales();
        buildAxis();
        // .. Rest of building blocks
    });
}

// Building blocks functions

function generateAccessor(attr) {
    function accessor(value) {
        if (!arguments.length) {
            return publicAttributes[attr];
        }
        publicAttributes[attr] = value;

        return chart;
    }

    return accessor;
}
```

```
    // API Generation
    for (let attr in publicAttributes) {
        if (
            (!chart[attr]) &&
            (publicAttributes.hasOwnProperty(attr))
        ) {
            chart[attr] = generateAccessor(attr);
        }
    }

    return exports;
};

export default chart;
```

In the previous listing, we have created accessors for the public properties. To do it, we looped over the "publicAttributes" object and called the "generateAccessor" helper function for each key. This function returns the generic accessor. We only need to attach the accessor to the chart object to make it available for users.

If we want to avoid repetition in the chart-sizing logic and axes creation, we can extract their code. Some library authors have opted for using base classes or objects, employing inheritance to share functionality. However, I recommend using helper functions instead. First, because it follows the motto "Composition over Inheritance." The second reason is that the fine granularity of helpers gives us more flexibility for the future.

D3.js-idiomatic and Well Accepted

We saw in Chapter 3 that there are many ways of approaching the creation of charts. Some of them end up abstracting D3.js code so much that the developer doesn't know that they are using the library. Others need so much D3.js code that developers sometimes think they are not using any abstraction.

The Reusable API covers a middle ground where the chart users need to use a bit of D3.js while the internals of the components are standard D3.js code. This fact makes it a low-friction choice for D3.js developers.

We first read about the Reusable API pattern in Mike Bostock's original post "Towards Reusable Charts" (`https://bost.ocks.org/mike/chart/`) in 2012. It hasn't changed a lot since then. Several libraries make use of this pattern, including the classic NVD3 (`http://nvd3.org/`) and Britecharts.

We also read about this pattern and their capabilities in books like *Developing a D3.js Edge* and *Mastering D3.js*. Multiple articles and blocks created by the D3.js community use it to encapsulate charts. Also, as we will see in Chapter 12, the Reusable API works well with other JavaScript libraries, as it is trivial to create wrappers for its charts.

Summary

In this chapter, we introduced the Reusable API. We saw how this encapsulation pattern works and how we can use it. We learned in which sense this abstraction solves the issues we mentioned in Chapter 2. We also discussed some of its drawbacks and how we can mitigate them. We saw why it is the closest to the D3.js way of coding and learned about its acceptance.

In the next chapter, we will see how to use the Reusable API to wrap the example code of the bar chart. We will create a production-ready chart that is reusable, configurable, and composable while keeping the output of the chart.

CHAPTER 5

Making the Bar Chart Production-Ready

In this chapter, we are going to refactor the standard D3.js bar chart we reviewed in the second chapter. It will become a professional-grade bar chart component. We will see how the Reusable API pattern proposed in the previous chapter allows us to encapsulate D3.js charts.

The resulting chart component is going to be extensible, and it will specify an explicit interface to interact with it. The Reusable API pattern supports that interface because we can create new getters and setters by adding a few extra lines of code.

The Path to Professional Code

We have seen the issues of example code when we use it outside of its demo purposes. In Chapter 3, we viewed different encapsulation strategies, and we justified the use of the Reusable API in Chapter 4. Using this abstraction is possible for us to transform example-based code into professional D3.js code. The question is, how can we do it?

In the present chapter, we follow the steps to transform our archetypal bar chart into professional code with the Reusable API. For that, we first set up the chart structure and dimensions. Then we create the building blocks of the chart and add configuration options including event handlers. Let's get into the details.

Setting Up the Chart Structure

We need to apply the core Reusable API pattern into the bar chart code of the original example (`http://bit.ly/pro-d3-bar-chart-v5`). We start by creating the root SVG element, give it dimensions, and produce a set of containers for our building blocks.

© Marcos Iglesias 2019
M. Iglesias, *Pro D3.js*, https://doi.org/10.1007/978-1-4842-5203-1_5

Creating the Core Pattern

The first step for creating a new module uses the code in Listing 5-1.

Listing 5-1. Core pattern

```
import * as d3 from 'd3';

function bar() {
    let data;

    function exports(_selection) {
        _selection.each(function(_data) {
            data = _data;

            // Main sequence here
        });
    }

    return exports;
};

export default bar;
```

Using the previous listing, when calling the bar module, we obtain in return a function that accepts a D3.js selection. This selection could be multiple, so the code loops over the selection using "each". This logic extracts from the DOM the data that we use for building our bar chart.

Observe that we are creating a variable called "data" that we keep private by setting a closure with the exports function. We later see how we can make private variables like this into a chart parameter that we can configure.

Building the Root Element

In the next step, we create the root SVG element that contains our chart. We write a function called "buildSVG" that is going to take the current D3.js selection and insert the root SVG element inside. In Listing 5-2 we show the code.

Listing 5-2. Building SVG

```
function buildSVG(container){
    if (!svg) {
        svg = d3.select(container)
            .append('svg')
            .classed('bar-chart', true);
    }
}
```

The "buildSVG" function is checking if there is a defined "svg" variable. If not, it creates a new SVG element inside the container and adds a class name of "bar-chart". We use this class to style our chart as well as to test it. We call this function by executing "buildSVG(this);" within the main sequence area of the pattern. Remember we must create a new variable with "let" called "svg" at the top of the primary function.

Giving Dimensions and Margins

Once we have a container, our chart needs to allow configurable dimensions. In the D3.js world, we usually add margins to our charts to make space to render our axes and chart labels.

Let's see how to do that, using the Margin Convention (http://bit.ly/pro-d3-margin-convention) popularized by Mike Bostock. We start by adding a default margin object to our chart, as well as the default sizes at the top of the "bar" function, as shown in Listing 5-3.

Listing 5-3. Declaring variables

```
let margin = {
    top: 20,
    bottom: 40,
    left: 40,
    right: 20
};
let width = 600;
let height = 400;
```

Next, we create two new variables that store the inner width and height of the chart. We exclude the margins when computing them. See Listing 5-4 for an example.

Listing 5-4. Setting height and width

```
...
let chartWidth;
let chartHeight;

function exports(_selection) {
    _selection.each(function(_data) {
        data = _data;
        chartHeight = height - margin.bottom - margin.top;
        chartWidth = width - margin.left - margin.right;

        // Main sequence here
        buildSVG(this);
    });
}
...
```

Inside "buildSVG", we use the "attr" command to set the original width and height as the sizes of our root SVG. In Listing 5-5 we have the finished "buildSVG" method.

Listing 5-5. Building the root SVG

```
function buildSVG(container){
    if (!svg) {
        svg = d3.select(container)
            .append('svg')
            .classed('bar-chart', true)
              .append('g')
                .attr(
                    'transform',
                    `translate(${margin.left},${margin.top})`
                );
    }
```

```
svg
    .attr('width', width)
    .attr('height', height);
}
```

Notice how in the previous code we have created a new group SVG element ("g") and translated it using the left and top margins of our chart. This process assigns the "svg" variable to the "g" element instead of to our original "svg" element.

This complex code is part of the Margin Convention. After applying this pattern, we can use the "svg" variable to operate with our chart without caring about the margins. The Margin Convention is super convenient. Before it became widespread, we had to add and subtract the margins all the time when positioning chart elements. With the Margin Convention, moving elements is more straightforward.

Creating Containers

In the previous listing, we employed the "g" element of SVG. Using "g" elements as containers makes it easier to move elements around. The SVG elements contained in a "g" element move with the container when it changes its position.

The same way, we benefit from having our SVG markup ordered in containers. For that reason, we create a function named "buildContainerGroups" in Listing 5-6.

Listing 5-6. Building containers

```
function buildContainerGroups(){
    let container = svg
      .append('g')
        .classed('container-group', true)
        .attr(
            'transform',
            `translate(${margin.left},${margin.top})`
        );

    container
      .append('g')
        .classed('chart-group', true);
    container
```

```
    .append('g')
      .classed('x-axis-group axis', true);
  container
    .append('g')
      .classed('y-axis-group axis', true);
}
```

In the preceding code, we moved the application of the Margin Convention into the container element. We are also adding containers for the chart group and both "x" and "y" axes. Next, you can see in Listing 5-7 how we call this function from "buildSVG".

Listing 5-7. Building containers

```
function buildSVG(container){
    if (!svg) {
        svg = d3.select(container)
            .append('svg')
            .classed('bar-chart', true);

        buildContainerGroups();
    }

    svg
        .attr('width', width)
        .attr('height', height);
}
```

Note how we call "buildContainerGroups" inside the branch that checks for the "svg" variable. We want to make sure we only generate the containers once, so this avoids re-creating them when updating the chart.

Creating Building Blocks

We saw how to use the Reusable API pattern to create the root SVG element of our chart. We also set the dimensions and margins of the chart and added containers to wrap the main elements. Now we need to generate the visualization blocks that form our chart. For that, we are going to create scales and axes, draw them, and render the bars of the visualization. Read on to see the code and explanation of it.

Creating Scales and Axes

To map the pixels available to the values we receive in our data, we need scales. These are functions that help us size and position the bars and axes of our chart. We follow the same pattern and create a "buildScales" function (Listing 5-8) that produces the scales.

Listing 5-8. Scales and axes

```
function buildScales(){
    xScale = d3.scaleBand()
        .rangeRound([0, chartWidth])
        .padding(0.1)
        .domain(data.map(getLetter));

    yScale = d3.scaleLinear()
        .rangeRound([chartHeight, 0])
        .domain([0, d3.max(data, getFrequency)]);
}
```

Here we are using the same code as in the archetypal bar chart of Chapter 2. In this case, we set the range and domain all at once, as we already have the data set. Before using this function, we need to create variables for "xScale" and "yScale". We also need to create the "getFrequency" and "getLetter" functions. They extract the frequency and letters from every data entry, as we see in Listing 5-9.

Listing 5-9. Extractor functions

```
const getFrequency = ({frequency}) => frequency;
const getLetter = ({letter}) => letter;
```

Once our scales are ready, we can build our chart's axes functions with the code in Listing 5-10.

Listing 5-10. Scales and axes

```
function buildAxes(){
    xAxis = d3.axisBottom(xScale);

    yAxis = d3.axisLeft(yScale)
        .ticks(10, '%');
}
```

Again, we must define the "xAxis" and "yAxis" variables at the top of our bar chart module. Listing 5-11 shows how we call these functions.

Listing 5-11. Scales and axes

```
function exports(_selection) {
    _selection.each(function(_data) {
        data = _data;
        chartHeight = height - margin.bottom - margin.top;
        chartWidth = width - margin.left - margin.right;

        // Main sequence here
        buildScales();
        buildAxes();
        buildSVG(this);
    });
}
```

Take into account that in the main sequence, the order we call the functions matters. In this case, as the axes depend on the scales, we should call "buildScales" first. In the next function calls, we must take into account the drawing order, especially relevant when working with SVG elements.

Drawing Axes

At this point, we can finally start drawing elements within our containers. We begin by rendering the axes using the "drawAxes" function. This method encapsulates the original chart's code, and uses our new group elements as the containers. Check Listing 5-12 for the implementation.

Listing 5-12. Scales and axes

```
function drawAxes(){
    svg.select('.x-axis-group.axis')
        .attr('transform', `translate(0,${chartHeight})`)
        .call(xAxis);
```

```
svg.select('.y-axis-group.axis')
    .call(yAxis)
      .append('text')
        .attr('transform', 'rotate(-90)')
        .attr('y', 6)
        .attr('dy', '0.71em')
        .attr('text-anchor', 'end')
        .text('Frequency');
}
```

By this point, you might be wondering about the extraneous indentation we are using in our D3.js code. In the D3.js world, there is a usual pattern to mark the operations that change selections. We do it with a double space instead of four spaces. This rule applies when we use "append", as the code that follows it is not applied to the initial selection (the axis group), but the appended element (the text). You can read more about this pattern in the "d3-selection" documentation (http://bit.ly/pro-d3-selections).

Drawing Bars

Finally, we arrived at the crucial step of the bar chart: drawing the bars. Let's see how we implement the "drawBars" function in Listing 5-13.

Listing 5-13. Bars and accessors

```
function drawBars(){
    // Select the bars, and bind the data to the .bar elements
    let bars = svg.select('.chart-group').selectAll('.bar')
        .data(data);

    // Enter
    // Create bars for the new elements
    bars.enter()
      .append('rect')
        .classed('bar', true)
        .attr('x', ({letter}) => xScale(letter))
        .attr('y', ({frequency}) => yScale(frequency))
        .attr('width', xScale.bandwidth())
        .attr('height', ({frequency}) => chartHeight - yScale(frequency));
```

```
// Exit
// Remove old elements by first fading them
bars.exit()
    .style('opacity', 0)
    .remove();
}
```

Here we have the famous and mind-bending enter-update-exit pattern. As we mentioned in Chapter 2, we won't go into the details of it. We refer you to "Thinking with Joins" (https://bost.ocks.org/mike/join/) and the "General Update Pattern" (http://bit.ly/pro-d3-eue-pattern) articles to solve any doubt about the pattern.

Note how we used ES2015 destructuring extensively. It is a useful feature to employ when working with D3.js code, as it makes our logic tighter and saves us keystrokes while preserving readability.

Adding Configurations

We have seen how to create a chart with the Reusable API. However, the chart is not configurable, and it doesn't allow other components to interact with it. In the next two sections, we see how to expose some of the chart attributes and listen to events happening within the module.

Creating Accessors

To allow users to change some of the default values we set in variables, such as the width, height, and margin, we need to put in place attribute accessors. As we saw in the previous chapter, these getters and setters look like the code in Listing 5-14.

Listing 5-14. Bars and accessors

```
exports.height = function(_x) {
    if (!arguments.length) {
        return height;
    }
    height = _x;

    return this;
};
```

When using this code, we call the "height" function. If we don't pass a value, the function returns the current value of height. If we pass an argument, it becomes the new value of the property.

The sum of all accessors establishes the API of our chart component. The primary gain of these methods is that we can use them to configure almost anything. We could expose a cleaning function, a callback, or any variable that changes the values of internal attributes. We could even allow passing in entire components like a legend if we choose that path.

Listening to Events

As an addition to the original bar chart example, we want to handle mouse events triggered by our users. To listen for events, we use a D3.js feature called dispatch (http://bit.ly/pro-d3-dispatch). This module acts as a publish-subscribe (http://bit.ly/pro-d3-pub-sub) messaging object, and we can implement the dispatcher with the code in Listing 5-15.

Listing 5-15. Events

```
// Dispatcher object that broadcast the 'customMouseOver' event
const dispatcher = d3.dispatch('customMouseOver');
```

The previous listing creates a dispatcher that listens and broadcasts the "customMouseOver" event. In Listing 5-16, we can see how we wire it with our bars within the "drawBars" function.

Listing 5-16. Wiring events

```
function drawBars(){
    // Select the bars, and bind the data to the .bar elements
    let bars = svg.select('.chart-group').selectAll('.bar')
        .data(data);

    // Enter
    // Create bars for the new elements
    bars.enter()
```

```
      .append('rect')
        .classed('bar', true)
        .attr('x', ({letter}) => xScale(letter))
        .attr('y', ({frequency}) => yScale(frequency))
        .attr('width', xScale.bandwidth())
        .attr('height', ({frequency}) => chartHeight - yScale(frequency))
        .on('mouseover', function(d) {
            dispatcher.call('customMouseOver', this, d);
        });

    // Exit
    // Remove old elements by first fading them
    bars.exit()
        .style('opacity', 0)
        .remove();
}
```

The added lines invoke any callbacks attached to the "customMouseOver" event. This logic means that when the user hovers over any of the bars, we pass the data of the specific bar and the context (this) to the callback.

To make these modifications useful, we need to attach callbacks to our custom event. In the code in Listing 5-17, we use an accessor to do that.

Listing 5-17. Events

```
exports.on = function() {
    let value = dispatcher.on.apply(dispatcher, arguments);

    return value === dispatcher ? exports : value;
};
```

This code applies the arguments to the dispatcher and returns the module (exports) to allow the method chaining. Let's see an example of how we use it in Listing 5-18.

Listing 5-18. Events

```
barChart.on('customMouseOver', function(event, data) {
    console.log('data', data);
});
```

We need this feature whenever we want to add a tooltip on an interactive legend. We can also use it to respond to the user hovering any of the bars in our bar chart. Moreover, it enables communication among components. Listening to events unlocks the composition of elements to build complex data visualizations.

Final Code

Finished the setup, building blocks, and configurations, we finally have a Reusable API chart working and ready to get tested. The finished code of our improved bar chart looks like the code in Listing 5-19.

Listing 5-19. Final bar chart

```
function bar() {
    // Attributes
    let data;
    let svg;
    let margin = {
        top: 20,
        right: 20,
        bottom: 30,
        left: 40
    };
    let width = 960;
    let height = 500;
    let chartWidth;
    let chartHeight;
    let xScale;
    let yScale;
    let xAxis;
    let yAxis;

    // Dispatcher object to broadcast the 'customHover' event
    const dispatcher = d3.dispatch('customMouseOver');
```

```
// Extractors
const getFrequency = ({frequency}) => frequency;
const getLetter = ({letter}) => letter;

function exports(_selection){
    _selection.each(function(_data){
        data = _data;
        chartHeight = height - margin.top - margin.bottom;
        chartWidth = width - margin.left - margin.right;

        buildScales();
        buildAxes();
        buildSVG(this);
        drawAxes();
        drawBars();
    });
}

// Building Blocks
function buildAxes() {...}
function buildScales() {...}
function buildSVG() {...}
function drawAxes() {...}
function drawBars() {...}

// API
exports.height = function(_x) {...}
exports.margin = function(_x) {...}
exports.on = function(_x) {...}
exports.width = function(_x) {...}

    return exports;
}

export default bar;
```

In the structure of this listing, we recognize four different sections. In the first block, we declare all the private and public variables of the module, as well as the helper functions. The next section is the core of the Reusable API pattern. In it, we extract the data from the selection and call the main sequence of functions that build the chart. The next two sections define those functions and the API of the module.

This structure makes it easy for developers to read and understand the chart code. We first give them a high-level view of the functionality in the main function. Then, we expose a lower abstraction level within each of the building and drawing functions.

When employing the chart, we use code such as the code in Listing 5-20.

Listing 5-20. Using the bar chart

```
let container = d3.select('.chart-container');
let barChart = bar();
let dataset = [...];

barChart
    .width(300)
    .height(200)
    .margin({
        left: 50,
        bottom: 30
    })
    .on('customMouseOver', function(event, data) {
        console.log('data', data);
    });

container.datum(dataset).call(barChart);
```

This code shows how we instantiate a bar chart module, configure it, and call it upon a D3.js selection that has a data set attached to it. The rendered chart looks like Figure 5-1.

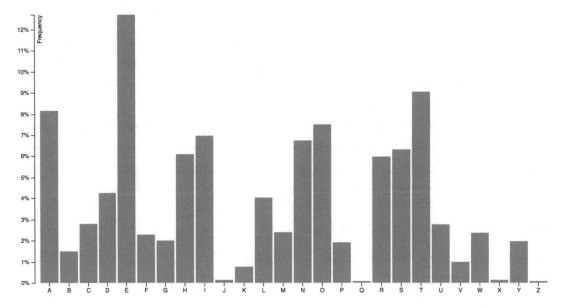

Figure 5-1. *Rendered bar chart*

We haven't changed a lot on the visual side, right? However, you know that in the inside, we made the chart a configurable, extensible, and structured piece of code. In successive chapters, we see how this structure allows us to test this chart and to extend it with other features quickly.

Summary

In this chapter, we have covered how to take a regular D3.js chart from a block example and turn it into a professional-grade chart module. We did it step by step, splitting the chart building and drawing logic into single responsibility functions.

Moreover, we have learned how structuring D3.js code with the Reusable API pattern helps with the readability of our charts. It also allows us to configure properties and wire events, making them reusable and composable.

In the next chapter, we will overview Britecharts, an open source charting library based on the Reusable API pattern. We will see how Britecharts follows this structure, making use of code helpers that supply valuable features.

CHAPTER 6

Britecharts

In this chapter, we are going to introduce Britecharts, a charting library based on the Reusable API. We will review how Britecharts helps developers by

- Representing different types of data with different charts

- Making it easy for users to read the charts using its support components

- Providing helpers to style charts and format numbers, dates, and axes

After reading this chapter, you will be familiar with the different charts Britecharts offers and when to use them. You will understand why we need support components, and you will be empowered to customize Britecharts by using its helper functions.

A Library for the Real World

In prior chapters, we have learned about the Reusable API and its benefits. This code pattern solves common problems of regular D3.js charts. We saw in the previous chapter how to move example code into the Reusable API format.

In the real world, developers need to create different kinds of visualizations for diverse data sets. Also, some need to target different media like the Web or print. Britecharts helps developers to visualize diverse data types by providing different chart types. It also provides support components to help final users to read the charts. As well, it offers helper functions for aiding in the formatting of charts, values, and axes.

Britecharts is a reusable charting library based on D3.js and the Reusable API. It allows the intuitive use of charts and components that we can compose, creating beautiful interactive visualizations.

© Marcos Iglesias 2019
M. Iglesias, *Pro D3.js*, https://doi.org/10.1007/978-1-4842-5203-1_6

We created Britecharts at Eventbrite in 2015. For us, it was a way to encapsulate some complex chart code and extract it into a different repository. The intention behind open sourcing Britecharts was twofold:

- Allowing developers and designers with little experience with D3.js to build great interactive charts with little effort.

- Proposing a structure for helping D3.js developers to create charts. We sought to systematize standards like the Reusable API and Test-Driven Development.

This proposed structure means that we can use Britecharts as a jumpstart for new charting libraries. For that, Britecharts offers two advantages:

- The infrastructure setup necessary to create charts with Test-Driven Development (TDD)

- A playground for polishing and testing charts, using our development sandbox and our demo pages

We also wanted to do all this with an eye for aesthetics so that users can have a beautiful chart working out of the box.

Visualizing Different Kinds of Data

When trying to extract insights from data sets, data visualization practitioners need different tools. Britecharts offers many charts so developers can describe different types of data in the best way for their visualization goals. In this section, we introduce those charts based on their uses and the data type they best represent.

Categorical Data

Categorical data is information organized into groups or categories. These could be quantities of different materials, sales on successive quarters, or percentages over a total share of items. Let's see which Britecharts charts work best for this kind of data.

Bar Chart

The bar chart or column chart is the most common chart for comparing categorical data. It shows how many elements of each category are there. Bar charts are easy to read for our eyes, as they use the longitude or height of the bars to compare quantities. In Figure 6-1, we show the horizontal version of this chart.

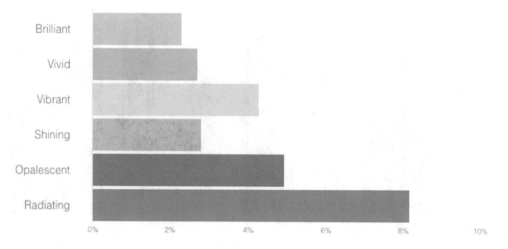

Figure 6-1. *Horizontal bar chart*

The horizontal is a robust variant of the bar chart as it allows more space for the category labels. We can use a legend and a mini-tooltip with this chart, as well as a brush component to filter data if necessary.

You can look at the code examples of the demo page (`http://bit.ly/bc-barchart-demo`) and the API reference (`http://bit.ly/bc-bar-api`), where we describe its options.

Grouped Bar Chart

We use grouped bar charts – also named multiset bar charts – to show multiple data sets visualized and grouped by categories or periods. This chart makes them easy to compare, and it works great up to a certain number of categories. See an example of a grouped bar chart in Figure 6-2.

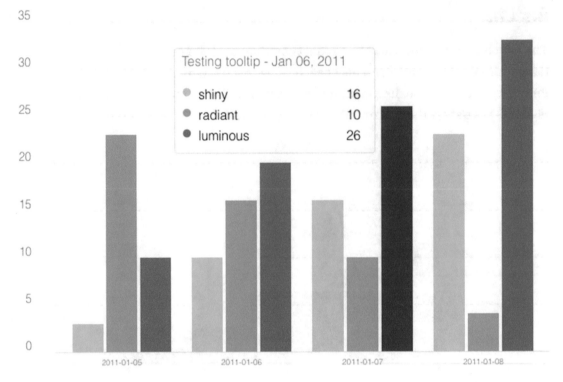

Figure 6-2. *Grouped bar chart*

Likewise the regular bar chart, grouped bar charts can also have a horizontal orientation. We usually show the grouped bar chart along a tooltip component if we deal with an interactive chart or with a legend if we plan to print our chart as well.

Navigate into these links to check the demos (`http://bit.ly/bc-grouped-bar-demo`) and API descriptions (`http://bit.ly/bc-grouped-bar-api`) of the grouped bar chart.

Stacked Bar Chart

The stacked bar chart shows multiple data sets one on top of the other. It illustrates graphically how one larger category is composed of other smaller categories. We can see an example in Figure 6-3.

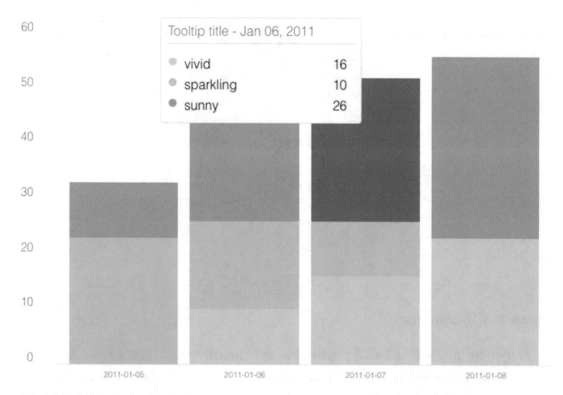

Figure 6-3. *Stacked bar chart*

See how the data set in the preceding chart is the same as in the grouped bar chart example. They only differ in that the stacked version also shows how much the aggregated categories sum. Likewise, this chart is usually employed along a tooltip like the one shown in Figure 6-3. Here is the demo (`http://bit.ly/bc-stacked-bar-demo`) and reference (`http://bit.ly/bc-stacked-bar-api`) for this chart.

Donut Chart

A donut chart is a variant of the pie chart, and as such, it shows proportions of a total. It reads better than pie charts. Donut's slices are easier to compare because they substitute slice areas for arc longitudes. See in Figure 6-4 an example of a Britecharts' donut, with the central interactive legend active for the largest slice.

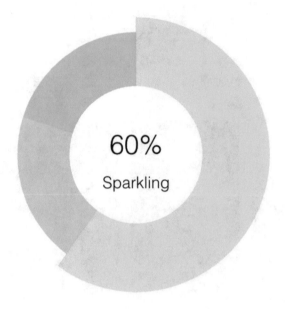

Figure 6-4. *Donut chart*

Our donut charts offer a wide variety of options (`http://bit.ly/bc-donut-api`), most of them requested by the community of Britecharts. Among them, you can keep a slice highlighted by default or on a fixed basis. We usually pair donut charts with vertical legends. They look great together, and we can synchronize them so we highlight the selected category on the legend when hovering over the donut slice. Play with these and other options by checking them in the donut's demos (`http://bit.ly/bc-donut-demo`).

Time Series

Time series data are values of a quantity obtained at successive times, frequently within symmetric intervals. We can use a line, stacked area, and sparkline charts from Britecharts to represent time series data.

Line Chart

The line chart is one of the most common chart types in some fields like financials and academia. It shows trends within time series data, and it can be mono- or multi-line. In Britecharts, we add a color gradient to the mono-line charts like the one in Figure 6-5.

Figure 6-5. *Line chart*

In the line chart, as well as in the other time series charts, we offer many options for formatting the x-axis. That means users can choose to have a double axis showing hours, days, months, or years. We review them more in detail when talking about the axis helper later in this chapter.

Line charts of multiple lines are usually shown together with legend components, and our tooltip component is also added on interactive versions. You can play with our demo (`http://bit.ly/bc-line-demo`), which includes a brush to filter data. Also, you can explore the API (`http://bit.ly/bc-line-api`) to become familiar with this famous chart.

Stacked Area Chart

Stacked area charts track multiple variables evolving over time. They also show the part-to-whole relationship and how each category contributes to the cumulative total. See a colorful example on Figure 6-6.

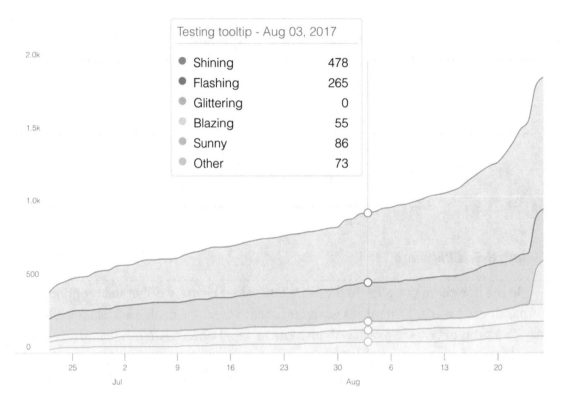

Figure 6-6. *Stacked area chart*

Developers use this chart to compare values and their contribution to the total. Sometimes we have used them to show the accumulation of the values. As shown in the previous figure, we pair it with our tooltip component and sometimes with a legend or brush.

It is a beautiful chart (`http://bit.ly/bc-stacked-area-demo`), and you can see that its options (`http://bit.ly/bc-stacked-area-api`) are pretty similar to those of the line chart.

Sparkline Chart

A lot smaller than the previous charts, sparklines are excellent to give a quick representation of statistical trends. Conceived to work inserted within a text paragraph, we can also use them in small dashboard widgets. See an enlarged example in Figure 6-7.

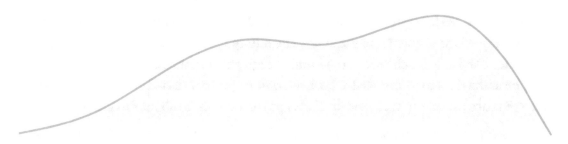

Figure 6-7. *Sparkline chart*

We built Britecharts' sparkline by overlapping an area and a line. We also gave both configurable color gradients. Note how it doesn't have axes so that we can place it in any small ubication, like a dashboard highlights section or the bottom of a user interface card. You can check its options (`http://bit.ly/bc-sparkline-api`) and demo (`http://bit.ly/bc-sparkline-demo`) in the documentation site of Britecharts.

Performance Metrics

Often, front-end developers that work on dashboards need to focus on a singular key metric. This metric includes references – like forecasts or industry averages. Britecharts provides one chart that helps with this data, the bullet chart.

Bullet Chart

Bullet charts are compact visualizations created by Stephen Few (`http://bit.ly/stephen-few`) that display performance metrics. They also render goals or estimations and the steps for milestones within the metric. See an example in Figure 6-8.

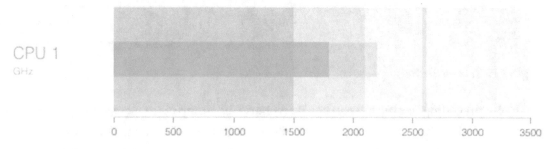

Figure 6-8. *Bullet chart*

As you can see in the figure, bullet charts are like bar charts with extra context. The primary value is in the center of the chart. The different color shades are qualitative ranges for that value (such as low, medium, or high performance). We can also use the last line at the right to fix our goal. Check our demos (`http://bit.ly/bc-bullet-demo`) and reference (`http://bit.ly/bc-bullet-api`) to learn more about this chart.

Variable Correlations

In academia, finding patterns in the relation of several variables is a prominent goal of data visualizations. In this line, scatter plots are usually the chart of choice. In this section, we introduce a scatter plot and another chart that we use to surface relationships.

Heatmap

A heatmap is a chart similar to tabular data which shows a broad relation between two variables. It displays a rating based on the value of every cell, using different colors or saturation of the same color to represent the rating. They usually have one category in the rows and another in the cells, and they are used to illustrate tabular data. In Figure 6-9 we see a heatmap with a week of data.

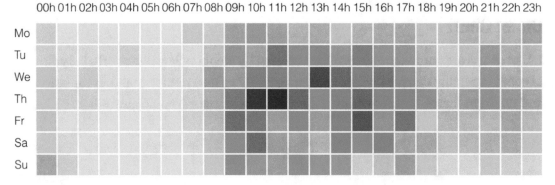

Figure 6-9. *Heatmap*

In the preceding figure, you can see Britecharts' heatmap chart representing a week worth of hourly data. In this specific example, the data is wind speed in the city of San Francisco. You can observe how most of the wind that week happened between nine in the morning and five in the afternoon. This pattern is the kind of insights that heatmaps are meant to surface.

Follow these links to see the demo (http://bit.ly/bc-heatmap-demo) and API reference (http://bit.ly/bc-heatmap-api) of this chart.

Scatter Plot and Bubble Chart

A scatter plot is a great visualization to identify correlations. It places points describing two variables in Cartesian coordinates, showing their relation. Scatter plots are famous in research, as they can surface different correlation types in the data. A bubble chart is a scatter plot with a third variable represented by the radius of the bubbles. We can see a bubble chart in Figure 6-10.

Figure 6-10. *Scatter plot/bubble chart*

We usually pair scatter plots with a mini-tooltip. In Britecharts, we use a Voronoi diagram (http://bit.ly/pro-d3-voronoi-ref) to divide the chart into sections. This partition allows us to highlight the closest data point when hovering over the chart with our mouse. Among the scatter plot options (http://bit.ly/bc-scatter-api), you can also choose to show a crosshair to inspect with greater accuracy. Visit the demo (http://bit.ly/bc-scatter-demo) to play with them.

Helping Reading Data Visualizations

Up to now, we have seen the variety of data that Britecharts helps to visualize. However, sometimes the charts by themselves are not enough to give a clear vision of the data. To mitigate this issue, Britecharts has components that developers can use to help in reading charts. Using the components we describe in this section, we can create rich data visualizations and dashboards.

Brush Chart

Occasionally the size of time-based data sets we want to visualize is vast. Long periods imply that users have a hard time diving into the details of the data. You can zoom into data by using Britecharts' brush component to filter time series. We do it by showing a mini representation of the whole data set alongside the main chart. This support graph enables the selection of sections of data with a simple drag-and-drop gesture. See Figure 6-11 for an example of a brush chart with a data section selected.

27   29   1   3   5   7   9   11   13   15   17   19   21   23   25   27   29   31   1

Figure 6-11. *Brush chart*

The brush chart allows for modifying our original selection. We can move the highlighted area horizontally by clicking and dragging to other sections of the data set. Users can also reset the filtering by clicking once somewhere else in the chart. Alternatively, developers can add a link to reset it as you can see in the demo (http://bit.ly/bc-brush-demo). The brush chart exposes specific custom events and options that you can find in the API reference (http://bit.ly/bc-brush-api).

Tooltip

In time series charts like the line chart or stacked area chart, sometimes it is not clear the exact value that the graphical elements represent. That is where using a tooltip for showing details in interactive charts is essential. We can use Britecharts' tooltip component with the line chart, stacked area chart, and grouped and stacked bar charts. It renders a configurable "title" line at the top and the data breakdown in the tooltip body. See an example in Figure 6-12.

Figure 6-12. *Tooltip*

You can see this support component in action when interacting with the line (http://bit.ly/bc-line-demo) or stacked area (http://bit.ly/bc-stacked-area-demo) chart demos. Among its options (http://bit.ly/bc-tooltip-api), there are many formatting configurations for values, titles, and dates.

Mini-Tooltip

When working with more straightforward data, Britecharts' fully fledged tooltip could be a bit overkill. That's why we use our newer tooltip in the bar and scatter plot/bubble charts. The mini-tooltip shows a title text row and one or two variables in a simpler design, as shown in Figure 6-13.

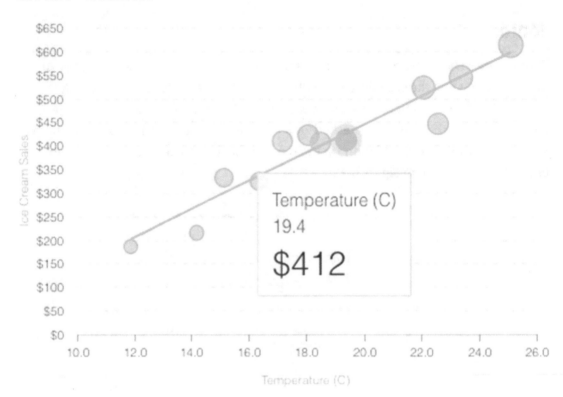

Figure 6-13. *Mini-tooltip*

The bar chart (`http://bit.ly/bc-barchart-demo`) and the scatter plot (`http://bit.ly/bc-scatter-demo`) demos are the best places to play with the mini-tooltip. For this simple component, we don't expose too many API options (`http://bit.ly/bc-mini-tooltip-api`).

Legend

Many charts benefit by being accompanied by a legend. Placing a legend alongside a chart helps with deciphering the meaning of colors, providing clarity. This benefit is especially crucial in print format or when using screenshots. You can use Britecharts' legend component along with any chart. It features two orientations: vertical and horizontal. In Figure 6-14 you can see the vertical shape.

●	Shiny	86.0000
●	Blazing	300.000
●	Dazzling	276.000
●	Radiant	195.000
●	Sparkling	36.0000
●	Other	814.000

Figure 6-14. *Legend*

You can take a look at the horizontal version in our donut chart demo (`http://bit.ly/bc-donut-demo`). There we make use of the legend's custom events to highlight categories when hovering slices. In the API reference (`http://bit.ly/bc-legend-api`), there are options for value formatting, marker sizes, and highlighting.

Formatting Charts

We have seen the charts that Britecharts supports out of the box. We also reviewed the components that developers can use to help in reading those charts. Often, engineers have specific requirements, or they are creating "niche" charts that only they use. Hence, they need to create their own charting libraries.

From the beginning, we made Britecharts a library that encourages developers to fork it in GitHub and create their charts. For these developers, we have extracted into helpers some logic used in our charts. In this section, we see some that deal with formatting and styling.

Styling Helpers

Britecharts is a project that puts much care in the styling of data visualizations. In that line, we provide some help to achieve beautiful looking charts. The "color," "load," and "filter" helpers are a set of constants that we expose to help developers style their visualizations.

Color

The "color" helper provides a list of objects expressing color palettes. They act as inspiration or out of the box color styling for your charts. This helper file includes

- **colorSchemas**: An object that contains color schemas. They are each an array of nine hexadecimal color values that you can apply directly or pick colors from.

- **colorGradients**: An object that contains two-element arrays representing the start and stop colors of a color gradient.

- **singleColors**: An object that contains arrays with one color as a single value.

We also include a list of these colors' "humanized" names. You can check them all in the colors demo page (`http://bit.ly/bc-color-demo`).

Filter

"filter" is a new helper we have been using lately to add nice SVG filtering effects to our chart markers. You can use it to add "glows," "blurs," and animations to elements in your charts.

Load

Lastly, the new "load" constant file exposes raw SVG markup elements. We can render these to show a "skeleton loader" version of our charts like the one in Figure 6-15 while users wait for the real chart to load.

Figure 6-15. *Line chart loading state (no animation)*

Britecharts integrates this feature into most charts and is particularly useful when loading large data sets asynchronously.

Formatting Helpers

During the evolution of Britecharts, we identified duplicated formatting logic. We extracted it, and now Britecharts provides helpers (`http://bit.ly/bc-helpers`) to aid in the formatting of axes, dates, numbers, and text.

Axis

The "axis" helper exposes the "getTimeSeriesAxis" function. It accepts the data, width, an optional axis-time combination, and an optional locale string. This function returns an object with minor and major formatting and tick values. We use these when drawing the x-axis of time series charts, as they can have a double axis (with a major and minor period). The axis-time combinations are pairs of date sizes, and they could be minute/hours, hours/days, days/months, and similar. You can read the code of this helper in Britecharts' repository (`http://bit.ly/bc-axis-helper`).

Date

The "date" formatting helper exposes some simple functions to help to work with dates. We included helpers like "addDays", "convertMillisecondsToDays", "diffDays", and "getLocaleDateFormatter" in this module.

Number

Our "number" helper contains some generic functions like "uniqueId", "isInteger", and "calculatePercent". It also contains two functions, "formatDecimalValue" and "formatIntegerValue", that are more attractive. They are our attempt to map different number sizes to the number formats that make sense for them. We use these functions to infer the right numeral format. Nevertheless, we usually allow the user to set a custom one because they are not perfect.

Text

Lastly, our "text" helper offers developers some text wrapping and sizing tools. They are necessary as rendering text in SVG is not as straightforward as with HTML. Among these, you can find "wrapText" and "wrapTextWithEllipses". These functions render text that wraps in many lines, and they are based on Mike Bostock's text wrapper function (`http://bit.ly/pro-d3-text-wrap`).

Chart Export

Sometimes users need an image file of the charts in the screen of their dashboards. That's why we created a chart export feature. We added this capability to Britecharts in the very beginning, as it was a request for Eventbrite's organizer reporting suite.

We distributed the logic for this feature between the "style" and the "export" helpers. The "style" helper allows serializing the styling of an SVG element. The "export" helper surfaces the "exportChart" function we use in most Britecharts modules. It accepts the SVG element, a filename, and a title for the picture. When called, it triggers a browser download of a ".png" image with the given filename.

Summary

In this chapter, we have seen how Britecharts helps developers building charts that represent different kinds of data. We learned how we can improve the exploration and interpretation of data by using components like brushes, tooltips, and legends. Finally, we discovered helpers that Britecharts offers to help developers to create charts or libraries.

In the next chapter, we will go hands-on creating a complete data visualization with Britecharts. We will use the charts and support components we have seen here to create a professional-looking chart.

CHAPTER 7

Using and Customizing Britecharts

In this chapter, we will create a complex data visualization using Britecharts. You will learn how to load Britecharts, instantiate and configure a simple chart, and plot an example data set. You will also discover how to make charts responsive.

Additionally, you will learn how to improve the chart's readability by adding a tooltip, a legend, and a brush to filter the data set. In the last section, you will find out how to customize the color schemas and CSS styling of the charts, so that they fit your tastes or requirements.

Introduction

Britecharts has been created to help developers consume and create D3.js charts. In the previous chapter, we saw how Britecharts helps developers in visualizing different data sets. It does it by providing a variety of charts that represent time series, categories, performance metrics, and variable correlations.

We have seen some support components like tooltips, legends, and brush charts that help to read the data in charts. Britecharts also provides them, and combined with helper functions, we can create our own charts and format them as needed.

Britecharts also allows creating complex data visualizations. We build them by rendering charts and using events to make the charts interact between themselves. In this chapter, we go over the steps necessary to create a complete and professional data visualization. We start by downloading Britecharts and creating a simple responsive chart. Then, we add a tooltip and legend. Finally, we allow filtering data through a brush chart and customizing the chart fonts and styling.

© Marcos Iglesias 2019
M. Iglesias, *Pro D3.js*, https://doi.org/10.1007/978-1-4842-5203-1_7

Downloading Britecharts

Before using Britecharts, we need to install the library. There are different ways we can load the source code in the browser. In this occasion, we are going to use a simple content delivery network (CDN) link to install it. For that, we create an HTML file and add the script tags in the header, as shown in Listing 7-1.

Listing 7-1. Downloading Britecharts

```
<script src="https://cdnjs.cloudflare.com/ajax/libs/d3-selection/1.2.0/d3-
selection.js"></script>

<script src=" https://cdn.jsdelivr.net/npm/britecharts@2.11.0/dist/bundled/
britecharts.min.js" type="text/javascript"></script>

<link rel="stylesheet" href="https://cdn.jsdelivr.net/npm/
britecharts@2.11.0/dist/css/britecharts.min.css" type="text/css" />
```

We are going to create a line chart and extend it with support charts, so we need to download the whole library bundle. Note that we also download "d3-selection". We use this module to create a selection and load the data in the container where we render the chart. We also need to load the CSS styling of Britecharts, and we do it similarly by accessing a CDN link.

This CDN approach works for us at the moment. If you decide to use Britecharts in your projects, you can follow the Installing Britecharts tutorial (`http://bit.ly/pro-d3-installing-britecharts`) to learn other ways of loading the library.

Creating a Simple Chart

Now that we have Britecharts available in our browser, we can start creating a chart. As we want to show some support components, we establish a simple and responsive line chart to build on top of it. In this first section, we describe how to build the line chart.

Setting Up a Container, Data set, and Chart

The initial step is creating a container, so first, we need to add a div element with a distinctive class to the DOM. Next, we can create our D3.js container selection using the "d3-selection" module. Finally, we instantiate a new chart by calling the function "line" inside the Britecharts object in the global namespace. See how this looks in Listing 7-2.

Listing 7-2. Setting up the container, data set, and chart instance

```
<body>
    <div class="line-container"></div>

    <script>
        const container = d3.select('.line-container');
        const lineChart = britecharts.line();

    </script>
</body>
```

We need a simple data set to render the line chart. We can find the right format of the data by visiting the API documentation for the line chart component (`https://bit.ly/bc-line-api`). We locate the data definition at the top of the page; in this case, it is a link labeled "LineChartData" (`http://bit.ly/bc-line-data`). In Listing 7-3 you can find an example.

Listing 7-3. Line chart required data schema

```
const lineData = {
    data: [
        {
            topicName: 'San Francisco',
            name: 1,
            date: '2017-01-16T16:00:00-08:00',
            value: 1
        },
        {
            topicName: 'San Francisco',
            name: 1,
            date: '2017-01-17T16:00:00-08:00',
            value: 2
        },
```

```
    {
        topicName: 'Oakland',
        name: 2,
        date: '2017-01-16T16:00:00-08:00',
        value: 3
    },
    {
        topicName: 'Oakland',
        name: 2,
        date: '2017-01-17T16:00:00-08:00',
        value: 7
    }
  ]
};
```

In this example data, we see the name of the topic ("topicName"), the id ("name"), a date in ISO format ("date"), and the quantity ("value"). For this chapter, we are going to use a similar data set, using a single topic named "Vivid" for this first simple chart.

Configuring and Rendering the Line Chart

Before configuring the chart, we figure out the container's size to apply it as the chart width. We use the "Element.getBoundingClientRect" method (`http://bit.ly/pro-d3-get-bounding-client-rect`) to find out the total dimensions of the HTML element wrapped in the D3.js selection. From it, we take the width attribute, as in Listing 7-4.

Listing 7-4. Finding out the container's width

```
const containerWidth = container.node().getBoundingClientRect().width;
```

Next, we only need to configure our bar chart by calling the accessors. We can read these in the line chart API reference (`https://bit.ly/bc-line-api`) page. In this chapter, we create a simple line chart with a height of 400 pixels and a width that depends on the container width. Configuring and rendering the line chart follows the same approach as we saw in Chapter 5, shown in Listing 7-5 for your convenience.

Listing 7-5. Configuring and rendering a simple line chart

```
lineChart
    .margin({bottom: 50})
    .height(400)
    .width(containerWidth);

container.datum(lineData).call(lineChart);
```

Notice how we tweaked a bit the bottom margin to allow space for our double x-axis (day and month) to render. The preceding code draws the chart in Figure 7-1.

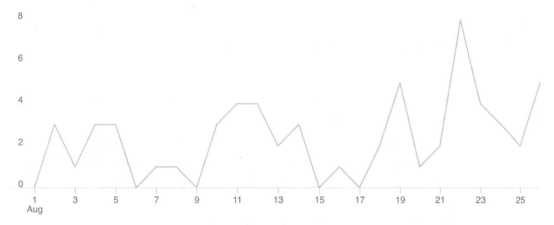

Figure 7-1. *Simple line chart*

As a reference, in Listing 7-6 is all the code inside the "<body>" tag of our HTML file.

Listing 7-6. Final code of the simple line chart

```
<div class="line-container"></div>

<script>
    // Instantiate line chart and container
    const lineChart = britecharts.line();
    const container = d3.select('.line-container');
    const containerWidth = container.node().getBoundingClientRect().width;

    // Create Dataset with proper shape
    const lineData = {...};
```

```
    // Configure chart
    lineChart
        .margin({bottom: 50})
        .height(400)
        .width(containerWidth);

    container.datum(lineData).call(lineChart);
</script>
```

Nothing too fancy, right? In real life though, nothing is that simple. Let's see how we make this line chart adapt to different viewport sizes.

Making the Chart Responsive

To make this chart responsive, we want to listen to the browser's "resize" event.

When the resize event triggers, we compute the container's width again, set it with the "width" accessor, and redraw the chart.

As the resize event triggers many times, we want to "throttle" the handler function. Throttling a function means to limit to the times the function gets called. This helps us avoid unnecessary renders. See the code in Listing 7-7 for an application of this pattern.

Listing 7-7. Responding to viewport width changes

```
const redrawChart = () => {
    const newContainerWidth = container.node() ? container.node().
    getBoundingClientRect().width : false;

    // Setting the new width on the chart
    lineChart.width(newContainerWidth);

    // Rendering the chart again
    container.call(lineChart);
};
// Create a throttled redrawChart function
const throttledRedraw = _.throttle(redrawChart, 200);

window.addEventListener("resize", throttledRedraw);
```

We need to load the Lodash (or Underscore) library so we can use its "throttle" function. We can do it with a CDN link in the HTML file's header, as shown in Listing 7-8.

Listing 7-8. Loading the Lodash library via CDN

```
<script src="https://cdnjs.cloudflare.com/ajax/libs/lodash.js/4.17.11/
lodash.min.js" type="text/javascript"/></script>
```

This approach is not the only way to avoid multiple successive calls. We can also listen to "requestAnimationFrame" to synchronize the execution of the handler.

We have created a responsive line chart! You can check the full code of this section in the book repository under the file: ch07/simple-line-chart.html.

Adding a Tooltip

Now that we have a line chart working, we add a tooltip to allow users to check the exact values on each date. We start by instantiating a new tooltip component (`https://bit.ly/bc-tooltip-api`).

In the next piece of code, we are going to bind the events triggering when users interact with the line chart to the tooltip component. The tooltip methods we are going to use are "show", "update", and "hide". Let's see how in Listing 7-9.

Listing 7-9. Instantiating and wiring the tooltip

```
const chartTooltip = tooltip();
//...

lineChart
    .margin({bottom: 50})
    .height(400)
    .width(containerWidth)
    .on('customMouseOver', chartTooltip.show)
    .on('customMouseMove', chartTooltip.update)
    .on('customMouseOut', chartTooltip.hide);
```

Following the previous code, we expect the tooltip to appear whenever the user passes his mouse over the chart. It should also hide when the mouse goes out of the area of the chart. Finally, the tooltip should update its values whenever the mouse moves within the limits of the chart.

We still have to attach the tooltip to the rendered line chart. For that, and only after we render the line chart, we draw the tooltip inside the "metadata-group" within the line. Let's see it in the code in Listing 7-10.

Listing 7-10. Rendering the tooltip

```
const tooltipContainer = d3.select('.line-container .metadata-group .hover-
marker');

tooltipContainer.call(chartTooltip);
```

After the previous code, we can see a tooltip like the one represented in Figure 7-2 when hovering the chart with our mouse.

Figure 7-2. *Line chart with tooltip*

The tooltip component shows the date of the hovered endpoint, the value of the topic in that date, and a configurable title. We can also modify the formatting of its values if necessary.

Drawing a Legend

Up to now, we have been working with a data set that contains only one topic. However, what would happen if we have two topics? In this section, and to make it a bit more interesting, we update our data to contain another set of entries. We add a legend component to show our users which line color corresponds to which topic.

First, we make a copy of the topic we already have and change some values. We named the new topic "Radiant," and due to our default color schema, it shows as a dark green line. See how we create the legend in Listing 7-11.

Listing 7-11. Instantiating the legend

```
<div class="legend-container"></div>

const chartLegend = britecharts.legend();
const legendContainer = d3.select('.legend-container');
```

In the previous code, we instantiate our legend component (https://bit.ly/bc-legend-api). The same way as we needed a container for the chart, we require another for the legend. To do it, we first create a div and then select the container with a D3.js selection and save the reference.

The legend is a component that requires a specific data shape. We check the legend data schema, which needs to be something like the code in Listing 7-12.

Listing 7-12. Legend data schema

```
[
    {
        id: 1,
        quantity: 2,
        name: 'glittering'
    },
    {
        id: 2,
        quantity: 3,
        name: 'luminous'
    }
]
```

As we want to show an inline legend, which doesn't show the quantity, we only need to pass an array with our topic names and an id. In Listing 7-13 is how we create that data.

Listing 7-13. Creating the legend data

```
const legendData = lineData.data.reduce(
    (accum, item) => {
        let found = accum.find((element) => element.id === item.name);
        if (found) { return accum; }

        return [
            {
                id: item.name,
                name: item.topicName
            },
            ...accum
        ];
    },
    []
);
```

Notice how we leverage "Array.prototype.find" to search for elements with the same id, so we can skip them when creating our new data array. This way, we end up with only one item per topic. Now, we are ready to configure and draw the legend, as we do in Listing 7-14.

Listing 7-14. Configuring and drawing the legend

```
chartLegend
    .width(containerWidth)
    .height(60)
    .isHorizontal(true);

legendContainer.datum(legendData).call(chartLegend);
```

In the preceding code, we have employed the container width to size the legend. This support component centers itself within the given width. You can see the rest of the options of the legend component in its API reference page (https://bit.ly/bc-legend-api). In our example, the resulting visualization is like the capture in Figure 7-3.

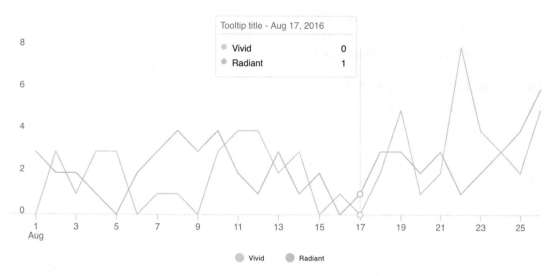

Figure 7-3. *Line chart with legend and tooltip*

The legend allows us to understand the chart without hovering with the mouse, and it is a crucial component when showing our charts in print format. You can see the completed code up to now in this HTML file: ch07/line-chart-with-legend.html.

Filtering Data with a Brush

Our example data is not extensive, but in theory, our line chart could render data sets of any size. A massive data set could be a problem, as we get into a position where the data points get too close, and our users can't see the details of the data. One way of fixing this is by allowing users to filter the data, and the way we do it visually is by using a brush chart.

In this section, we go over the process of adding a brush chart to our visualization, allowing to drag and drop a section of the data to focus in that period.

Creating the Brush Chart

Let's first add the brush chart container div to the DOM and instantiate the brush chart and its container. We do this in Listing 7-15.

Listing 7-15. Instantiating the brush

```
<div class="brush-container"></div>

const chartBrush = britecharts.brush();
const brushContainer = d3.select('.brush-container');
```

Now, as we did before, we check the brush chart API (http://bit.ly/bc-brush-api) and its data schema (http://bit.ly/bc-brush-data). The passed data needs to look like the one in Listing 7-16.

Listing 7-16. Brush data schema

```
[
    {
        value: 1,
        date: "2011-01-06T00:00:00Z"
    },
    {
        value: 2,
        date: "2011-01-07T00:00:00Z"
    }
]
```

So, to get this data shape, we will need to do some modifications to our line chart data. We want to sum up both topic values, creating a single set of data entries. See Listing 7-17 for an approach to do this using Array.reduce.

Listing 7-17. Generating the brush data

```
const lineDataCopy = JSON.parse(JSON.stringify(lineData));
const brushData = lineDataCopy.data.reduce(
    (accum, d) => {
        let found;

        accum.forEach((item) => {
            if (item.date === d.date) {
                item.value = item.value + d.value;
                found = true;
```

```
            return;
        }
    });

    if (found) {
        return accum;
    }

    return [d, ...accum];
    },
    []
);
```

In the preceding reducer function, we sum up the values to have an aggregate of them while avoiding duplicating dates.

Note how we used the "parse" and "stringify" methods of the JSON object to create a deep copy of our data set. Using this method, we turn the array into a string with "stringify." Then, we use "parse" to do the contrary, turning the string into an object. This object is new, so we avoid issues related to mutating data that we could experience when creating shallow array copies in JavaScript.

This approach copies deeply nested arrays and objects; however, it can be resource consuming for the CPU. We should use it sparingly and only when necessary. Also, mind that this method won't convert JavaScript values that don't have an equivalent in JSON, like "NaN" or "Infinity." Lastly, if you use "Lodash," you can use the "clone" function with the deep flag as "true" to get a slightly more performant data copy.

Now we are ready to configure and render our brush using the familiar pattern in Listing 7-18.

Listing 7-18. Configuring and drawing the brush

```
chartBrush
    .width(containerWidth)
    .height(100)
    .xAxisFormat(chartBrush.axisTimeCombinations.DAY_MONTH)
    .margin({top:0, bottom: 40, left: 50, right: 30});

brushContainer.datum(brushData).call(chartBrush);
```

Notice that we are setting the x-axis format to a constant called "DAY_MONTH" within the "axisTimeCombinations" object. This code renders a simple brush chart like the one in Figure 7-4.

Figure 7-4. *Simple brush chart*

The "xAxisFormat" option is a way for us to select a date format that works for our data. In this case, it is the day of the month, as the default one (hours) was showing the same hour every day, not giving us much value.

Wiring the Brush Events

At this moment, the brush component only serves as an overview of the aggregated data in our data set. What we want to do is, when we drag and drop a section of the brush, re-render the line chart with the selected part of our data set.

For that, we listen to the "customBrushEnd" event on the brush, which returns the period of the brush selection. We use the beginning and end of that period to filter our original data. Finally, we apply it to the line chart and re-render. In Listing 7-19 is the code for it.

Listing 7-19. Wiring the brush event with the line chart

```
chartBrush
    .width(containerWidth)
    .height(100)
    .xAxisFormat(chartBrush.axisTimeCombinations.DAY_MONTH)
    .margin({ top: 0, bottom: 40, left: 50, right: 30 })
    .on('customBrushEnd', ([brushStart, brushEnd]) => {
        if (brushStart && brushEnd) {
            let filteredLineData = filterData(brushStart, brushEnd);

            container.datum(filteredLineData).call(lineChart);
        }
    });
```

This results in a data visualization where we can focus on different sections of the data and use our tooltip to see the values on individual days. See how it looks like in Figure 7-5.

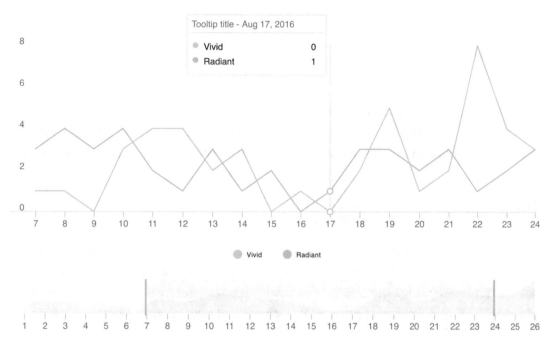

Figure 7-5. *Line chart with brush, tooltip, and legend*

In Listing 7-20 is the filtering logic for your reference.

Listing 7-20. Data filtering logic

```
const isInRange = (startDate, endDate, {date}) => new Date(date) >=
startDate && new Date(date) <= endDate;

const filterData = (brushStart, brushEnd) => {
    // Copy the data
    let lineDataCopy = JSON.parse(JSON.stringify(lineData));

    lineDataCopy.data = lineDataCopy.data.reduce(
        (accum, item) => {
            if (!isInRange(brushStart, brushEnd, item)) {
                return accum;
            }
```

```
            return [...accum, item];
        },
        []
    );

    return lineDataCopy;
};
```

where "isInRange" finds out if a date is within the given range and "filterData" returns a new array with the original data contained in the date period. Examine the full code of this section in this file of the book repository: ch07/line-chart-with-brush.html.

Customizing the Styles

We have created a beautiful visualization; however, users have specific branding and styling needs for their charts. In this section, you learn how you can use Britecharts' color schemas to change the chart's colors or customize your own. We also see how to override the CSS styles that come with Britecharts and how to update the fonts.

Applying a Color Palette

Let's look at some customization options we have available for Britecharts. The first ones are color schemas and gradients. You can find a visual showcase in our Color Palettes demo page (http://bit.ly/bc-color-demo).

Starting with the line chart, we want to customize our visualization's colors. For that, we first need to load our color schemas by accessing its object in Britecharts' bundle. Then, we can set the color schemas of the line chart and legend by calling "colorSchema" as in Listing 7-21.

Listing 7-21. Applying color schemas to line and legend

```
const colorSchemas = britecharts.colors.colorSchemas;

...

lineChart
    .margin({ bottom: 50 })
    .height(400)
```

```
.width(containerWidth)
.colorSchema(colorSchemas.orange)
.on('customMouseOver', chartTooltip.show)
.on('customMouseMove', chartTooltip.update)
.on('customMouseOut', chartTooltip.hide);

...

chartLegend
    .height(60)
    .width(containerWidth)
    .colorSchema(colorSchemas.orange)
    .isHorizontal(true);
```

That renders a line chart with orange lines shown in Figure 7-6.

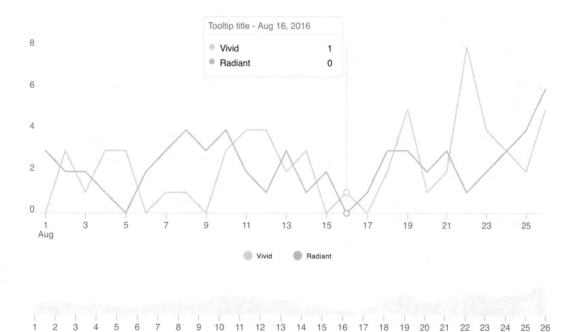

Figure 7-6. *Line chart with orange color schema*

The different color palettes we provide in Britecharts are ubicated within the "colorSchemas" object. When we take a look at the palette code, we find that they are just an array of nine hexadecimal values. For example, the default Britecharts palette looks like the array in Listing 7-22.

Listing 7-22. Color palette example

```
// Britecharts palette
["#6aedc7", "#39c2c9", "#ffce00", "#ffa71a", "#f866b9", "#998ce3"]
```

So, if you want to customize your chart's color palette, you only need to pass arrays of hexadecimal colors into the "colorSchema" accessors.

Overriding Default Styles

Whenever we want to change the font family, font sizes, or any other styling of our charts, we can do so by creating CSS override declarations. As an example, let's change the font of our data visualization.

We'll begin by looking for a new font in Google Fonts (`https://fonts.google.com/`). I am a fan of the font "Oswald," so let's add it to our code by including this link tag in the header, as we do in Listing 7-23.

Listing 7-23. Loading a Google font

```
<link href="https://fonts.googleapis.com/css?family=Oswald:600"
rel="stylesheet">
```

Now, we need to set up a style override declaration. For that, we can inspect our SVG elements with the browser's dev tools. In this case, we see that the "font-family" attribute is set within the "britechart" class. To override it, we need to add a "style" tag after the link that loads the default Britecharts styling and, inside the tag, include the code in Listing 7-24.

Listing 7-24. Overriding the font styles

```
<style>
    .britechart,
    .tick text {
        font-family: 'Oswald', sans-serif;
    }
```

```
.brush-chart rect.brush-rect.handle {
    fill: #ffa71a;
}
</style>
```

This CSS code overrides the "font-family" definition for both the whole chart and the specific tick text of our axes. We are also updating the brush handle colors. In the code in Listing 7-25, we style the brush gradient as well.

Listing 7-25. Styling the brush

```
// Configure and draw the brush chart
chartBrush
    .width(containerWidth)
    .height(100)
    .gradient(colorSchemas.orange.slice(0, 2))
    .xAxisFormat(chartBrush.axisTimeCombinations.DAY_MONTH)
    .margin({ top: 0, bottom: 40, left: 50, right: 30 })
    .on('customBrushEnd', function ([brushStart, brushEnd]) {
        if (brushStart && brushEnd) {
            let filteredLineData = filterData(brushStart, brushEnd);

            container.datum(filteredLineData).call(lineChart);
        }
    });
```

See how we are picking the first two colors of the orange color palette to set the gradient. This modification results in the data visualization in Figure 7-7.

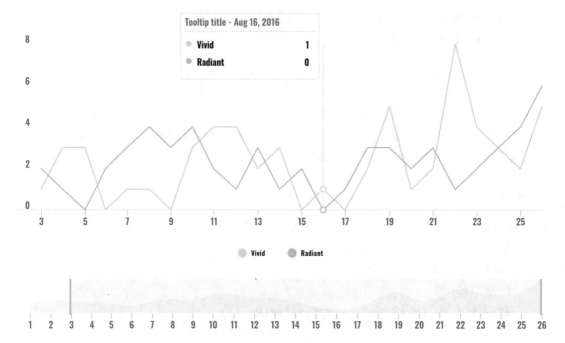

Figure 7-7. *Line chart with orange colors and custom font*

We can follow the same steps to style most of Britecharts' components. One warning is that, given that Britecharts is an SVG-based library, the styling of SVG elements is sometimes different. You can check out this SVG styling guide (`http://bit.ly/pro-d3-svg-styling`) to make sure you are updating the right properties.

Summary

In this chapter, we have seen how to load Britecharts with a CDN link and to draw a simple chart with the library. We understood how we could use support components like the legend and tooltip to provide extra visual information about our charts.

We also learned how we can use the brush chart to provide a high-level view of our data set, and we saw how to configure it to filter the data of our primary chart. Lastly, we discovered how to customize the styles of our data visualization.

In the next chapter, we will go over the setup and process necessary to extend a Britecharts chart. In successive chapters, we will talk more in-depth about testing our charts and how we get our charts ready to ship and release.

CHAPTER 8

Extending a Chart

This chapter is about increasing the functionality of charts and components. You will see how to modify a Britecharts chart so that it covers your requirements. We also follow the development process from setup, code creation, and testing to the code submission and approval.

You will learn how to contribute to Britecharts and, hence, to any open source software (OSS) project present in GitHub.

Introduction

In the previous chapter, we have seen how we can use Britecharts to create a simple line chart. We extended that chart by adding support components like a legend and a tooltip. These components, along with a brush chart that enables data filtering, made it easier for the final users to read the data in our visualization. We also saw how Britecharts enables many charts and support element combinations out of the box.

However, Britecharts doesn't provide all the possible features that users could need. So, how can we extend Britecharts components to enable for more specific use cases and functionalities?

In this chapter, we follow the steps to get ready to contribute to Britecharts; update a chart with extra functionality and send a pull request with our changes to GitHub, making it possible to get those changes reviewed and added to the library.

Getting Set Up to Contribute

To start contributing to Britecharts, we need to set up our machine to develop with the library. In this section, we learn what is a project "fork" and how to create it. We also create a branch and run the project documentation, demos, and sandbox in our development machine.

© Marcos Iglesias 2019
M. Iglesias, *Pro D3.js*, https://doi.org/10.1007/978-1-4842-5203-1_8

Setting Up the Repository

The first thing we do to start developing in Britecharts is the setup of our copy of the library. With this copy, we can download the latest changes in the code and propose changes to the original project. We do this by creating a "fork," that is, a copy of Britecharts linked to our personal GitHub account.

In the rest of the chapter, I assume you have a GitHub account, although if you don't, GitHub will prompt you to create one. We start by creating our fork of Britecharts by clicking the "fork" button at the top right corner of the repository page (`https://github.com/eventbrite/britecharts`).

Then, we clone the repository in our machine by clicking the "Clone and download" green button and copying the URL. Now we can open a new terminal window and type "`git clone https://github.com/<OUR_HANDLE>/britecharts.git`" to create a folder with the latest version of Britecharts.

After downloading, we can get into the repository by typing "cd britecharts". We need to pull the library dependencies by running "yarn install". If you don't have yarn in your machine, follow the instructions in their site (`https://yarnpkg.com/en/docs/install`) to download and install this package manager utility. Yarn requires Node.js, and at the time of writing, we are using version 12.2.0, that you can find in `https://nodejs.org/en/download/`.

Running Docs and Demos

Now that we have the project installed in our machine, we can try to run the demos we see on the library homepage. This process also allows us to inspect the documentation and play around with our development sandbox.

To generate the demos and build the library documentation, we need to run "yarn start" while being in the root of the repository folder. This script does three things for us:

1. Compiles the project's documentation, bundling our demo files with the CSS styles and HTML files. It also runs a JSDoc task to generate the API reference, something we'll talk about in detail in Chapter 11.

2. Starts a development server that enables the navigation into the demos and documentation site. This server includes hot module reload, allowing developers to see their changes without refreshing the page.

3. Initiates another development server that exposes a "Sandbox" environment on the 8002 port. This tool allows developers to test their charts with different configurations and data sets.

Once we have the docs running, we can navigate the API of each chart and see some examples under the "Demos" drop-down section. I recommend using the demos along with the sandbox as a testing platform when modifying the charts, as we see later in this chapter.

Creating a Branch

Now we are ready to start coding. However, we don't want to make changes in our fork's "master" branch. We prefer to create a branch where we can add our changes and later decide if we want to contribute them to the project. If you are not familiar with git, you can learn some of the basics in this quick guide (`http://bit.ly/pro-d3-git-guide`).

When forking a project and downloading it to our machine, we create a copy of the project that points to our forked repository. As Britecharts evolves, we want to establish a connection with the original code so that we can incorporate its latest changes to our copy. We do this by creating an "upstream" branch, following these steps:

In our local master, we set the upstream to `https://github.com/eventbrite/britecharts.git` by running

```
$ git remote add -track upstream https://github.com/eventbrite/britecharts.git
```

We make sure it worked by running "git remote -v"; afterward, we should read something like this:

```
$ git remote -v
origin      git@github.com:Golodhros/britecharts.git (fetch)
origin      git@github.com:Golodhros/britecharts.git (push)
upstream    git@github.com:eventbrite/britecharts.git (fetch)
upstream    git@github.com:eventbrite/britecharts.git (push)
```

Now, we can pull the most recent changes from the original project by running "git pull --rebase upstream master". This command fetches the latest changes in Britecharts and places our changes on top of them.

Now that our repository is fully prepared, we can create a new branch to contain our changes. When working with Britecharts, branch names should be prefixed, depending on the type of modification we want to introduce. We prefix with "feat-" for new features, "fix-" for bug fixes, and "ref-" for refactors, that is, code modifications that don't affect the user experience. To create a new branch, we run the command "git checkout -b [fix|feat|ref]-<OUR_BRANCH_NAME>", for example, "git checkout -b feat-grouped-bar-duration-accessor". This command creates a new branch and moves us into it.

Modifying a Chart

We are ready to change Britecharts components within our git branch. We want to follow the recommended approach to contribute, but we still don't know how. This section walks us through the process of modifying a chart, starting from a failing test, making it pass with new code, and reviewing it using the docs and demos.

Creating Our First Failing Test

The Britecharts team has created its components following a "Tests First" approach, and they encourage contributors to keep the same process. However, we can also write tests later; it is up to us.

For a Test-Driven Development (TDD) workflow, the process of modifying a chart begins by creating a branch as we did in the previous section. Then, after running the demos with "yarn start", we can navigate to the demo of the chart we are modifying. To begin developing, we want to open two files in our text editor:

> The chart file, which we can find in the "src/charts" folder or in "src/charts/helpers" if we need to change a helper function

> The chart test file, which lives in the "test/specs" folder of our repository

Now we are ready to write a failing test for the feature we want to add. In this case, and as an example, let's imagine that we want to add an accessor to configure the "animationDuration" property of the grouped bar chart. For that, we first create an API test following the pattern present in the test file (Listing 8-1).

Listing 8-1. Grouped bar chart accessor test

```
it('should provide an animationDuration getter and setter', () => {
    let previous = groupedBarChart.animationDuration(),
        expected = 600,
        actual;

    groupedBarChart.animationDuration(expected);
    actual = groupedBarChart.animationDuration();

    expect(previous).not.toBe(expected);
    expect(actual).toBe(expected);
});
```

We place the preceding code in the test file, within the "describe" clause labeled as "API". The code gets the current value of the property and stores it in the "previous" variable. Then we set the new value to the property and reread it. Finally, we assert that the initial value didn't change and that the latest set value is the expected. If some of this code is confusing, don't worry, we address chart testing in the next chapter.

In a new terminal, we run the "yarn test" command to see the test running. This command opens a new Chrome browser window and runs the tests and test coverage tasks for us. At this point, we expect only one test to fail. If there are more, we should stash our changes and try it again, making sure the initial state of our branch is correct.

Adding a New Accessor

Now that we have a failing test, we can write the code that makes this test pass. For that, we open the chart file located in "/src/charts/", and following Britecharts' API guidelines (http://bit.ly/bc-api-guidelines), we add our new accessor. In the API guidelines, we can find some considerations when naming variables depending on their types and function.

Let's see the code that makes the previous test pass in Listing 8-2; it should be pretty familiar now.

Listing 8-2. Grouped bar chart animationDuration accessor

```
exports.animationDuration = function (_x) {
    if (!arguments.length) {
        return animationDuration;
```

```
    }
    animationDuration = _x;

    return this;
};
```

As we saw in Chapter 4, this function returns the current value of the "animationDuration" property if it is called without an argument. If the user passes an argument, the accessor sets it as the new value of the property.

In this case, the code added is trivial, but sometimes it could get complicated. That is where working with an excellent test suite becomes vital. We can feel safe that Britecharts' test suite fails if we mess up something, so we are empowered to refactor our code until it feels clean and efficient.

Updating Demo and Documentation

We have our new test passing thanks to the accessor code we added to the chart. We know that the API works, but does it apply correctly to the animation? To make sure this happens, we can apply the new accessor and verify it in our demos. We also need to update our documentation; let's see how.

Britecharts' API reference gets generated from comments included in the source code. We are going to dive deeper on how in Chapter 11, and here we only review what's necessary to keep the docs up to date. For that, we add a JSDoc-type comment to the accessor definition in Listing 8-3. Thanks to this comment, the correct documentation gets generated when we run "yarn run docs".

Listing 8-3. Grouped bar chart animationDuration accessor with comments

```
/**
 * Gets or Sets the duration of the bar grow animation
 * @param  {Number} _x=1000   Desired animationDuration for chart
 * @return {Number | module}  Current animationDuration or chart module to
chain calls
 * @public
 */
exports.animationDuration = function (_x) {
    if (!arguments.length) {
        return animationDuration;
```

```
    }
    animationDuration = _x;

    return this;
};
```

The first two lines of the previous comment describe what the accessor does and specify the type of the input argument. Note that we also state what the default value for that attribute is by using "_x=<defaultValue>".

The next line describes the possible outputs of the function call. The "@public" tag tells that this is a public method, and so it should be included in the documentation. This behavior contrasts to functions labeled as "@private" that we kept out of the docs. We learn more about the different comment tags in Chapter 11.

To see this comment in our docs, we need to run the docs script "yarn run docs" and visit "http://0.0.0.0:8001/module-Grouped-bar.html". We should see the descriptor for the new accessor as in Figure 8-1.

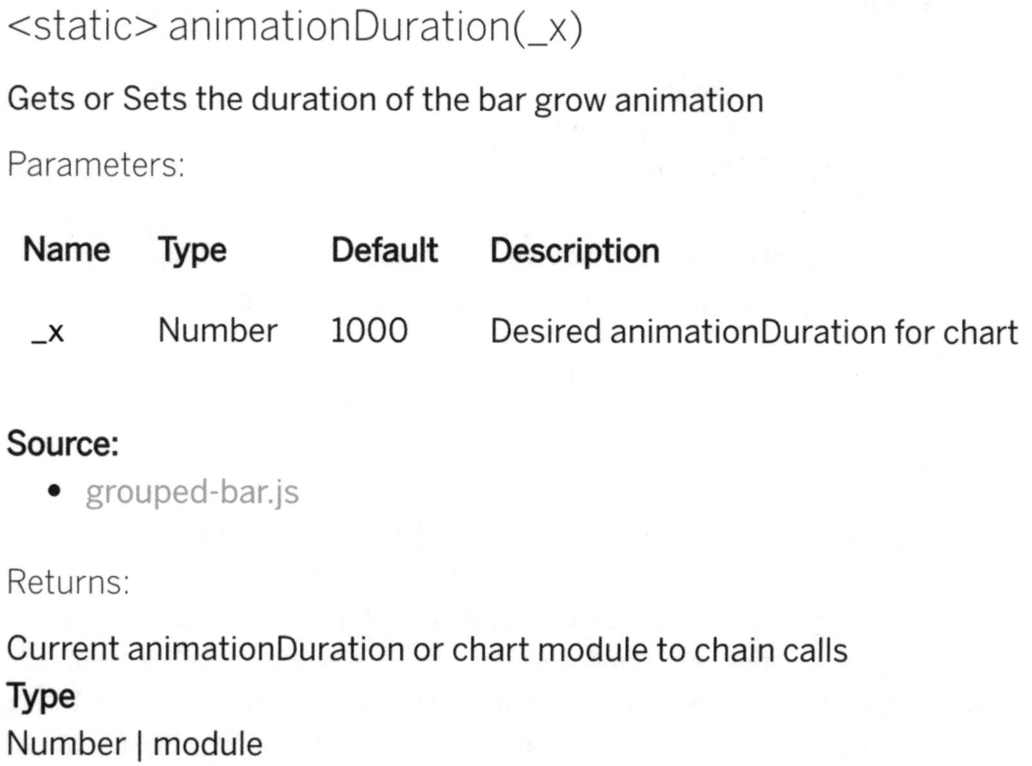

`<static> animationDuration(_x)`

Gets or Sets the duration of the bar grow animation

Parameters:

Name	Type	Default	Description
_x	Number	1000	Desired animationDuration for chart

Source:
- grouped-bar.js

Returns:

Current animationDuration or chart module to chain calls

Type

Number | module

Figure 8-1. *Accessor API description*

We should check manually that the new accessor changes the duration of the animation. For doing it, we have two options: using the demos or working with the development sandbox.

To use the demos, we open the demo JavaScript file for the chart (demos/src/demo-grouped-bar.js) and, picking the first example chart, add the configuration shown in Listing 8-4.

Listing 8-4. Grouped bar chart demo with animationDuration

```
// GroupedAreChart Setup and start
groupedBar
        .tooltipThreshold(600)
        .animationDuration(2000)
        .width(containerWidth)
        .grid('horizontal')
        .isAnimated(true)
        .groupLabel('stack')
        .nameLabel('date')
        .valueLabel('views')
        .on('customMouseOver', function() {
            chartTooltip.show();
        })
        .on('customMouseMove', function(dataPoint, topicColorMap, x,y) {
            chartTooltip.update(dataPoint, topicColorMap, x, y);
        })
        .on('customMouseOut', function() {
            chartTooltip.hide();
        });
```

Note how we choose a long duration (2 seconds) to notice the feature in action. In some cases, we can also add a new demo to the file if necessary.

The second way to verify our change is by using the development sandbox. This sandbox section is a handy feature for contributors; however, it is not polished enough to expose it to final users. We can access the sandbox by navigating to "http://0.0.0.0:8002/" after running "yarn run start". The initial state of the sandbox is that of a dashboard with a chart, configuration, and chart data widgets shown in Figure 8-2.

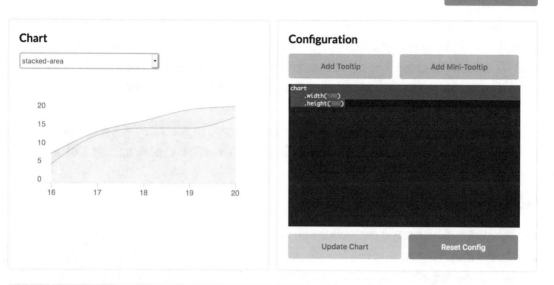

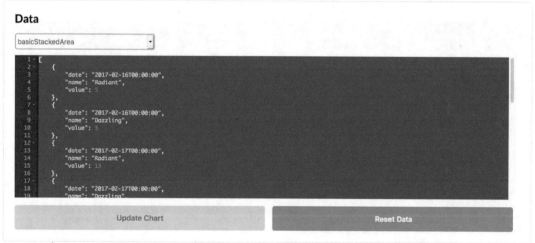

Figure 8-2. *Development sandbox for Britecharts*

To test our grouped bar chart accessor, we select the chart on the top left select box. We change the configuration on the top right widget so that it includes the "animationDuration" the same way we did with the demo. Finally, by clicking the "Update Chart," we should see our chart update with the new animation duration.

The sandbox section is still a work in progress, and the Britecharts team is planning to flesh it out more before incorporating it to the regular documentation.

Sending a Pull Request

In the previous sections, we have created a chart modification in a branch in our fork of Britecharts. Now, we need to tell the core maintainers that we have done that work and that we want to propose it as a permanent addition to the library. For that, we should send a pull request. A pull request, or PR, is the way developers contribute to projects when working on OSS.

Here we describe the process of creating a new pull request and get it merged into the library. However, we start with an explanation of GitHub's issue tracker feature.

Using the Issue Tracker

GitHub offers to all hosted projects a bug tracker feature that helps to organize and monitor issues. We can find the bug tracker in the "Issues" tab beside the default "Code" tab on the top left of the repository page. The user interface looks like Figure 8-3.

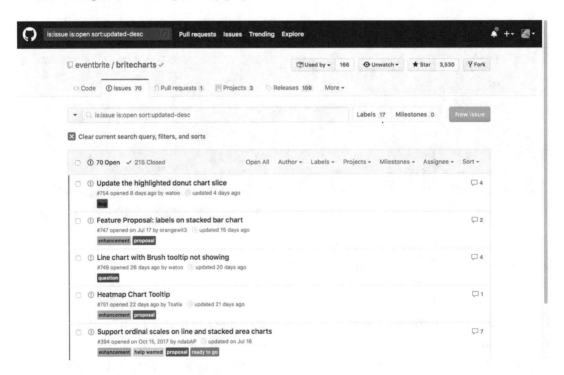

Figure 8-3. *GitHub's issue tracker screen*

This feature is not only aimed to manage bugs, as we can use it to get user feedback, accept feature proposals, and organize tasks.

The Britecharts team uses the "Issues" tab extensively, and they receive notifications whenever a user creates a new issue or comment. In this link (`http://bit.ly/bc-open-issues`), we can see all open issues, classified with different labels such as

> **bug**: Outstanding bugs and issues related to the charts, demos, and documentation of the library.

> **proposal**: Feature proposals that the team employs to get an idea of what users think is missing on Britecharts and to decide the roadmap based on the popularity of each proposal.

> **good first issue**: Tickets aimed for newcomers to the library or OSS in general. These are usually simple fixes and enhancements tailored to make it easy for developers to start contributing.

There are always tickets labeled as "good first issue," and they are a great starting point if a developer wants to get started. Contributors may also take on any issues that don't currently have an assignee and are labeled as "ready to go."

Before sending a pull request with significant changes, it is useful to search the issues for similar requests. If there aren't any, contributors can create a new ticket to discuss the potential improvements they want to make before doing any development work. This step saves throwaway work and frustrations.

Creating a Pull Request

Let's assume we have created a ticket about our "animationDuration" accessor and got the green light of Britecharts' maintainers. Once we have a branch that we want to contribute, we need to create a PR to suggest the addition of the code. In this section, we talk about the steps we should follow.

The first action is to make sure that our branch is up to date with the current code of the library. For that, once we are happy with our code and have a commit with it, we go to the "master" branch by running "git checkout master" and update it with the latest changes using "git pull upstream master". This command updates our local master branch with the master branch of the original Britecharts project on Eventbrite's repository.

Then, we go back to our feature branch with "git checkout feat-grouped-bar-duration-accessor" and execute "git rebase master". This request extracts our changes and pulls them aside. Then, it updates our feature branch with the latest commits on master and puts back our changes on top of them. Sometimes, there are conflicts, and we need to be careful when resolving them.

In the next step, we push our feature branch to our fork by running "git push origin feat-grouped-bar-duration-accessor". This command creates a new remote branch in our forked repository. To create a new pull request with this branch, we only need to navigate to the original Britecharts repository (`https://github.com/eventbrite/britecharts`) and accept the prompt to create a new PR.

Britecharts' pull requests use a GitHub feature called "Pull Request Templates." This feature shows us prefilled text along with companion comments that describe the information suggested for each section. When filling this template, it is crucial to add a link to the original issue, so that both issue and pull request get closed at the same time.

After submitting our PR, we only have to wait for somebody in the core team of Britecharts to address it. They might comment on it, giving their approval or suggesting changes to make the code better. Once we finish this process, they will merge the code into Britecharts, so our contribution is available in the next release.

Summary

In this chapter, we have followed the path to contribute to Britecharts. We started setting us up for success with the right repository configuration, creating a new branch and running the docs, demos, and tests on our local machine.

After that, we modified the grouped bar chart, adding a new accessor following a test-first approach. We also updated the docs and made sure our change worked using the chart demo and the development sandbox. Finally, we introduced GitHub's issue tracker and walked over the process of sending a new pull request to Britecharts.

In the next chapter, we will dive deeper into testing Britecharts components. We introduce the tools we use, create tests for our features and accessors, and also test the events triggered by our components. The following chapters will deal with building the library, releasing it to the public, and creating a generated documentation.

CHAPTER 9

Testing Your Charts

In Chapters 3 and 4, we saw some D3.js code encapsulation strategies and chose an abstraction: the Reusable API. Later in Chapter 5, we saw how to transform standard D3.js code into production-ready Reusable API components. However, to produce a real professional chart, we need to supply unit tests to the component.

In this chapter, we follow the steps to redo our example bar chart in a Test-Driven Development (TDD) way, achieving a professional chart with ample test coverage. We'll cover the creation of unit tests for Reusable API components and go over the process of preparing a simple development environment to test our charts, creating the test setup and fixtures, and designing the different kind of tests we need to have full test coverage.

Read on to learn how to test the rendered elements of our components, how we can test the events dispatched from charts, and how we can test the accessor functions that form its API.

Setting Up the Test Environment

To get started with testing the D3.js code, we need to set up the development environment. In Britecharts, we have been using the **Karma test runner** (https://karma-runner.github.io/) and **Jasmine** (https://jasmine.github.io/) as the testing framework. Its main benefits are

- **Debugging in a real browser**, in contrast with JS-DOM-based solutions that only run in the command line. This factor is essential in D3.js development, as sometimes it is not clear what we render in the DOM.

- Running tests in **different browsers** like Chrome, Firefox, Safari, Opera, Internet Explorer, and PhantomJS as a headless browser.

© Marcos Iglesias 2019
M. Iglesias, *Pro D3.js*, https://doi.org/10.1007/978-1-4842-5203-1_9

Still, not everything is good news. We must make some tradeoffs, so as drawbacks, we count

- Needs to **start a real browser** to run tests. We mitigate this issue when running the tests in "watch" mode, as we start the browser only once.

- **Slower tests** than non-DOM solutions. This is unavoidable, but likely not a significant issue given the volume of tests that a charting library would have. As an example, Britecharts' 700 tests get to run in less than 10 seconds.

Setting up the bundler, test runner, and configuration is often a bit of a hassle. In the next chapter, we will dive deep in the transpilation and bundling of the library with Webpack and Babel. However, focusing only on tests, there is a project that allows to set up Webpack, Karma, and Jasmine in minutes by using several defaults. The open source project is called "Karmatic" (`http://bit.ly/pro-d3-karmatic`), and in this section, we'll see how to use it to create our tests.

Setting Up Karmatic

We begin by installing our dependencies using Yarn. If you don't have it installed, you can visit their docs (`http://bit.ly/pro-d3-yarn`) to get you started. Then, we create a new folder in our machine and, inside it, initialize a new NPM package by running "npm init". After filling in the prompts that ask us about the name, author, description, and license for our package, we can get started with the development.

We install Karmatic by running "yarn add -D webpack karmatic". Then, following the docs in the project repo, we add a "test" script in the "package.json" file that calls the "karmatic" command. Examine it in Listing 9-1.

Listing 9-1. Test script in package.json

```
"scripts": {
    "test": "karmatic",
    "test:watch": "karmatic watch --no-headless",
}
```

After it, we can execute a test file suffixed with ".test.js" by running "yarn run test". We could see it working by creating a dumb test file and run it with Karmatic. Let's do it by typing the code in Listing 9-2.

Listing 9-2. Dumb test to make sure our testing framework runs

```
describe('Dumb Test', () => {
    it('should pass', () => {
        expect(true).toEqual(true);
    });
});
```

Running Karmatic includes Webpack bundling of all our tests and source files, which we can find in the "/dist" folder under the file named "bundle.js". We also get to see an Istanbul report for code coverage in the command line. We have the possibility of executing our tests using Puppeteer, a headless version of Chromium (i.e., a Chromium browser without the graphical interface). When we run "yarn test", we get the command-line output we see reflected in Listing 9-3.

Listing 9-3. Running the dumb test in the command line

```
  Dumb Test
    ✓ should pass
Executed 1 of 1 SUCCESS (0.002 secs / 0.002 secs)

=============================== Coverage summary ===========================
Statements     : 100% ( 0/0 )
Branches       : 100% ( 0/0 )
Functions      : 100% ( 0/0 )
Lines          : 100% ( 0/0 )

============================================================================
✨  Done in 4.50s.
```

Note how the coverage summary gives a 100% result, as it doesn't think there is any code to cover yet. From now on, we are going to run "yarn test:watch" instead of "yarn test". This command keeps Karma watching for changes in our tests or source code, rerunning the tests every time we save our files.

Creating the Test Fixtures

To create meaningful tests, we need to set up the DOM fixture and the data we are going to use. For the latter, we utilize the same data set Mike Bostock used in his seminal blog post about creating a bar chart (`https://bost.ocks.org/mike/bar/`) and also employed in our example of Chapter 5.

For creating the DOM container fixture, which we are using as the root of our chart, we follow the examples of Karmatic, as noted in Listing 9-4.

Listing 9-4. DOM fixture with Karmatic

```
const data = [
  {
    "letter": "A",
    "frequency": 0.08167
  },
  ...
];

describe('Bar Chart', () => {
    let barChart;
    let container;

    beforeEach(() => {
        const fixture = '<div id="fixture"><div class="container"></div>
        </div>';

        // adds an html fixture to the DOM
        document.body.insertAdjacentHTML('afterbegin', fixture);
    });

    // remove the html fixture from the DOM
    afterEach(function() {
        document.body.removeChild(document.getElementById('fixture'));
    });
});
```

In this code, we create a string containing a div with id "fixture" and, within it, a div with class "container". We use the DOM function "insertAdjacentHTML" to insert the container HTML before each test run. Lastly, we use the "afterEach" clause to remove the fixture container following each test finalization. This process makes sure we start every test with a blank slate. We also create placeholder variables to store our chart and container instances. You can find the code for this step in the "step-1-fixtures" branch of the testing demo repository (`http://bit.ly/pro-d3-testing-1`).

Creating the Rendering Tests

Once we established our environment to test with Jasmine and have our data and DOM fixtures ready to use, we can get started writing our tests. However, where should we start? As we are already familiar with the code, we are going to approach testing in a TDD way, starting with the chart container.

Rendering the Root Element

In the last years, I have followed an approach to testing Reusable API components that groups the tests into "Render," "Lifecycle," and "API" tests. Using this approach, we begin by adding a "Render" describe clause and creating an instance of our bar chart, as stated in Listing 9-5.

Listing 9-5. Render describe clause

```
describe('Render', () => {
    beforeEach(() => {
        barChart = bar();
        container = d3.select('.container');

        container.datum(data).call(barChart);
    });

    afterEach(() => {
        container.remove();
    });
});
```

As usual, we create a bar chart and a container selection, mixing them with the data by calling the selection "datum" function and applying the chart to it using "call". After each test, we remove the container from the HTML by calling "remove" on the container selection.

The first test we write and fail is the one checking the existence of the chart root element. You can see it in Listing 9-6.

Listing 9-6. Test for the root element existence

```
it('should render a basic bar chart', () => {
    const expected = 1;
    const actual = container.select('.bar-chart').size();

    expect(actual).toEqual(expected);
});
```

In this test, we find out how many elements with a class "bar-chart" are present in the HTML, and we expect there is only one.

I want to pause here for a moment and talk about the structure of this test, as we follow a similar approach for the rest of the tests in this chapter. When creating tests, I am inspired by the writings of Eric Elliott about testing (`http://bit.ly/pro-d3-elliot-tests`). On them, he advises against the use of sophisticated assertions using matchers. Those are "magical" most of the times, and ultimately, non-necessary, as using the standard "toEqual" matcher works in 99% of the cases.

In the tests in this chapter, we follow a similar pattern. First, we describe what we expect it will happen in the label of the "it" clause. Then, we create an "expected" variable where we note the expected result. The "actual" variable holds what we get from the tested behavior. Finally, our assertion is always the same: "expect(actual).toEqual(expected)".

Following this strategy has several benefits:

- Our tests have identical structures, making them easy to read and maintain and also more predictable.

- We don't need to learn by heart different matchers with different names depending on the test runner. That means our tests look the same whether we use Jasmine, Jest, Mocha and Chai, Tape, AVA, or any other test runner and assertion library combination.

- We can copy/paste one test, change the first three lines, and have a new test.

Now, returning to our first test, it should be failing by now. To make it pass, we create a file for our chart, named "barChart.js" and import it on our test file. In this chart file, we import the D3.js library, and we use the code in Listing 9-7.

Listing 9-7. Creating the container

```
import * as d3 from 'd3';

function bar() {
    // Variable creation

    function exports(_selection){
        _selection.each(function(_data){
            data = _data;
            chartHeight = height - margin.top - margin.bottom;
            chartWidth = width - margin.left - margin.right;

            buildSVG(this);
        });
    }

    function buildSVG(container){
        if (!svg) {
            svg = d3.select(container)
              .append('svg')
                .classed('bar-chart', true);
        }
        svg
            .attr('width', width)
            .attr('height', height);
    }

    return exports;
};
export default bar;
```

Remember, we analyzed this code in Chapter 5. On it, we set up the primary function of the Reusable API pattern and call "buildSVG", which creates an SVG root element with the class "bar-chart". Note that we omitted the creation of the rest of the variables for the sake of brevity. You can see the final code in the book repository under the file "ch09/bar-chart-code.js". Our test should be passing now.

Rendering Container Groups

In the next test, we check for the presence of the "<g>" elements that hold the different elements of our chart. We create a new "describe" clause within the "Render" describe to hold all the tests related to these container groups. In Listing 9-8, we show all the tests at once, although I recommend adding them one by one, making them pass before adding the next.

Listing 9-8. Container group tests

```
describe('groups', () => {
    it('should create a container-group', () => {
        const expected = 1;
        const actual = container.select('g.container-group').size();

        expect(actual).toEqual(expected);
    });

    it('should create a chart-group', () => {
        const expected = 1;
        const actual = container.select('g.chart-group').size();

        expect(actual).toEqual(expected);
    });

    it('should create a x-axis-group', () => {
        const expected = 1;
        const actual = container.select('g.x-axis-group').size();

        expect(actual).toEqual(expected);
    });

    it('should create a y-axis-group', () => {
        const expected = 1;
        const actual = container.select('g.y-axis-group').size();

        expect(actual).toEqual(expected);
    });
});
```

Notice how we follow the same pattern, checking for the size of the selections that wrap each CSS selector. The code that makes these tests pass is in Listing 9-9.

Listing 9-9. Rendering the container groups

```
function buildSVG(container){
    if (!svg) {
        svg = d3.select(container)
          .append('svg')
            .classed('bar-chart', true);

        buildContainerGroups();

    }
    svg
        .attr('width', width)
        .attr('height', height);
}

function buildContainerGroups(){
    let container = svg
      .append('g')
        .classed('container-group', true)
        .attr(
            'transform',
            `translate(${margin.left},${margin.top})`
        );

    container
      .append('g')
        .classed('chart-group', true);
    container
      .append('g')
        .classed('x-axis-group axis', true);
    container
      .append('g')
        .classed('y-axis-group axis', true);
}
```

See how we make the most of the "buildContainerGroups" function to add the containers one by one. After adding this code to "barChart.js", our container tests should pass.

Rendering Axes

When writing tests for our component, we only create tests for the code that has public effects. That means that either the code is public via the component API or it renders something in the HTML. That's why we can't test the creation of the bar chart X and Y scales, we only test the drawing of the axes, as the code in Listing 9-10.

Listing 9-10. Testing the axes drawing

```
describe('axis', () => {
    it('should draw an X axis', () => {
        const expected = 1;
        const actual = container.select('.x-axis-group.axis').size();

        expect(actual).toEqual(expected);
    });

    it('should draw an Y axis', () => {
        const expected = 1;
        const actual = container.select('.y-axis-group.axis').size();

        expect(actual).toEqual(expected);
    });
});
```

In these tests, grouped as well within a describe clause, we check that our component draws into X and Y axes. The code in Listing 9-11 makes this test pass.

Listing 9-11. Code to draw the axes

```
const getFrequency = ({frequency}) => frequency;
const getLetter = ({letter}) => letter;

function exports(_selection){
    _selection.each(function(_data){
        data = _data;
```

```
        chartHeight = height - margin.top - margin.bottom;
        chartWidth = width - margin.left - margin.right;

        buildScales();
        buildAxes();
        buildSVG(this);
        drawAxes();
    });
}

function buildAxes(){
    xAxis = d3.axisBottom(xScale);

    yAxis = d3.axisLeft(yScale)
        .ticks(10, '%');
}

function buildScales(){
    xScale = d3.scaleBand()
        .rangeRound([0, chartWidth])
        .padding(0.1)
        .domain(data.map(getLetter));

    yScale = d3.scaleLinear()
        .rangeRound([chartHeight, 0])
        .domain([0, d3.max(data, getFrequency)]);
}

function drawAxes(){
    svg.select('.x-axis-group.axis')
        .attr('transform', `translate(0,${chartHeight})`)
        .call(xAxis);

    svg.select('.y-axis-group.axis')
        .call(yAxis)
          .append('text')
            .attr('transform', 'rotate(-90)')
            .attr('y', 6)
            .attr('dy', '0.71em')
```

```
            .attr('text-anchor', 'end')
            .text('Frequency');
}
```

Adding this code to our bar chart file, along with the required variables, makes our axes tests pass. Note how we extracted a couple of small functions that get the frequency and letter values from our data entries.

Rendering Bars

We got to the last tests for rendering our chart and the whole point of the component, rendering the bars. This is a straightforward test, checking for the number of bars that we draw and comparing them to the number of data entries in our original data set. See Listing 9-12 for the test code.

Listing 9-12. Test for the bars

```
it('should draw a bar for each data entry', () => {
    const expected = data.length;
    const actual = container.selectAll('.bar').size();

    expect(actual).toEqual(expected);
});
```

This test fails until we add the code in Listing 9-13 to our chart file.

Listing 9-13. Code for drawing the bars

```
function exports(_selection){
    _selection.each(function(_data){
        data = _data;
        chartHeight = height - margin.top - margin.bottom;
        chartWidth = width - margin.left - margin.right;

        buildScales();
        buildAxes();
        buildSVG(this);
        drawAxes();
        drawBars();
```

```
    });
}

function drawBars(){
    let bars = svg.select('.chart-group').selectAll('.bar')
        .data(data);

    // Enter
    bars.enter()
      .append('rect')
        .classed('bar', true)
        .attr('x', ({letter}) => xScale(letter))
        .attr('y', ({frequency}) => yScale(frequency))
        .attr('width', xScale.bandwidth())
        .attr('height', ({frequency}) => chartHeight - yScale(frequency));

    // Exit
    bars.exit()
        .style('opacity', 0)
        .remove();
}
```

With this last test, we are done checking for the different elements on our component. However, there is yet another rendering test we can create. As we commented on Chapter 4 about the Reusable API, one of the benefits of this pattern is the ability to reload the chart with different data. Let's add a test checking for this use case, like the one in Listing 9-14.

Listing 9-14. Checking for data reload

```
describe('when reloading with a different dataset', () => {
    it('should render in the same svg', () => {
        const expected = 1;
        const newDataset = alternativeData;
        let actual;

        container.datum(newDataset).call(barChart);
        actual = container.selectAll('.bar-chart').size();

        expect(actual).toEqual(expected);
    });
```

```
it('should render six bars', () => {
    const expected = 6;
    const newDataset = alternativeData;
    let actual;

    container.datum(newDataset).call(barChart);
    actual = container.selectAll('.bar-chart .bar').size();

    expect(actual).toEqual(expected);
});
});
```

In these tests, we reload our bar chart with an alternative data set, which is a similar one with only six data entries. The tests make sure that we reuse the SVG root element and that we render only six bars. On the contrary of the previous tests, these pass initially, as the logic in the Reusable API pattern includes this feature.

You can find the final code at this stage of the process in the "step-2-rendering" branch of the demo repository (`http://bit.ly/pro-d3-testing-2`). At the root of the same repository, you can find an HTML file named "index.html", which you can open by running "yarn start" and visiting "localhost:1234".

Testing Events

We just saw how to build a bar chart step by step using a test-driven approach. Our resulting chart has all the visual elements we would expect in a chart of its type, but it doesn't allow for any interactivity. We can't make it interact with other charts or user interface elements either. To solve this, in this section, we add event listeners to several events on each bar: mouse over, mouse out, mouse move, and mouse click.

Testing Mouse Hover

The first event we test for is the hover event on a bar. For that, we create a new "describe" clause labeled as "Lifecycle". Within this section, we write a "beforeEach" and "afterEach" functions, creating and cleaning the bar chart instance. In Listing 9-15, we see an example of the test and its setup.

Listing 9-15. Testing the mouse over event

```
describe('Lifecycle', () => {
    beforeEach(() => {
        barChart = bar();
        container = d3.select('.container');

        container.datum(data).call(barChart);
    });

    afterEach(() => {
        container.remove();
    });

    describe('when hovering a bar', () => {
        it('should trigger a callback once on mouse over', () => {
            const expected = 1;
            const firstBar = container.selectAll('.bar:nth-child(1)');
            const callbackSpy = jasmine.createSpy('callback');
            let actual;

            barChart.on('customMouseOver', callbackSpy);
            firstBar.dispatch('mouseover');
            actual = callbackSpy.calls.count();

            expect(actual).toEqual(expected);
        });
    });
});
```

In the previous "it" clause, we select the first bar in our chart using the "nth-child" CSS pseudo-class selector. We use Jasmine to create a "Test Spy" – which is a function we employ to record the method calls to it by the system under test. In this case, we test the component's "customMouseOver" event. Then, we use the yet to be created "on" accessor to set our spy as the callback function of the custom event. We trigger the hover event on the first bar using the "dispatch" method of the D3.js selection and check how many calls did our spy receive.

To make the previous test pass, we need to create the dispatcher object and pass it the custom event name. Then, we create an "on" accessor and dispatch the event on every "mouseover" event on the bar elements. In Listing 9-16 we can see the code.

Listing 9-16. Enabling event triggering on the bar chart

```
const dispatcher = d3.dispatch('customMouseOver');

//...

function drawBars(){
    let bars = svg.select('.chart-group').selectAll('.bar')
        .data(data);

    // Enter
    bars.enter()
      .append('rect')
        .classed('bar', true)
        .attr('x', ({letter}) => xScale(letter))
        .attr('y', ({frequency}) => yScale(frequency))
        .attr('width', xScale.bandwidth())
        .attr('height', ({frequency}) => chartHeight - yScale(frequency))
        .on('mouseover', function(d) {
            dispatcher.call('customMouseOver', this);
        });

    // Exit
    bars.exit()
        .style('opacity', 0)
        .remove();
}
//...

exports.on = function() {
    let value = dispatcher.on.apply(dispatcher, arguments);

    return value === dispatcher ? exports : value;
};
```

Notice how we call the "customMouseOver" custom event when we trigger the "mouseover" event in any of the bars. The "on" accessor allows us to set callback functions by calling it with the custom event name as the first argument and the callback as the second. If we call "on" passing only the custom event, we get back the current callback function assigned to that custom event.

Now our test passes. However, we want to pass the data entry information to the custom event callback. In Listing 9-17, we see the test which, added inside the describe clause, checks for that data point.

Listing 9-17. Test looking for the data point information

```
it('should trigger the callback with the data entry as argument', () => {
    const expected = data[0];
    const firstBar = container.selectAll('.bar:nth-child(1)');
    const callbackSpy = jasmine.createSpy('callback');
    let actual;

    barChart.on('customMouseOver', callbackSpy);
    firstBar.dispatch('mouseover');
    actual = callbackSpy.calls.first().args[0];

    expect(actual).toEqual(expected);
});
```

Note how we search inside our test spy looking for the first argument passed to the first call made to it. In the next code snippet, labeled Listing 9-18, we have the code that makes this test pass.

Listing 9-18. Passing down the data entry

```
//...
// Enter
bars.enter()
  .append('rect')
    .classed('bar', true)
    .attr('x', ({letter}) => xScale(letter))
    .attr('y', ({frequency}) => yScale(frequency))
    .attr('width', xScale.bandwidth())
```

```
    .attr('height', ({frequency}) => chartHeight - yScale(frequency))
    .on('mouseover', function(d) {
        dispatcher.call('customMouseOver', this, d);
    });
```

We could pass more arguments to the event, such as the mouse location, the chart dimensions, or any other parameter we need. For that, we would add more arguments separated by commas after the "d" variable.

Testing More Mouse Events

We just saw how to test and implement a mouse event in our bar chart. We can add more, and both the tests and code to implement them are identical to the previous. In this section, we add events for mouse move, mouse out, and mouse click events.

For the sake of brevity, we show their three describe clauses in Listing 9-19.

Listing 9-19. Tests for mouse over, out, and click events

```
describe('when moving over a bar', () => {
    it('should trigger a callback once on mouse over', () => {
        const expected = 1;
        const firstBar = container.selectAll('.bar:nth-child(1)');
        const callbackSpy = jasmine.createSpy('callback');
        let actual;

        barChart.on('customMouseMove', callbackSpy);
        firstBar.dispatch('mousemove');
        actual = callbackSpy.calls.count();

        expect(actual).toEqual(expected);
    });

    it('should trigger the callback with the data entry as argument', () => {
        const expected = data[0];
        const firstBar = container.selectAll('.bar:nth-child(1)');
        const callbackSpy = jasmine.createSpy('callback');
        let actual;
```

```
        barChart.on('customMouseMove', callbackSpy);
        firstBar.dispatch('mousemove');
        actual = callbackSpy.calls.first().args[0];

        expect(actual).toEqual(expected);
    });
});

describe('when moving out of a bar', () => {
    it('should trigger a callback once on mouse out', () => {
        const expected = 1;
        const firstBar = container.selectAll('.bar:nth-child(1)');
        const callbackSpy = jasmine.createSpy('callback');
        let actual;

        barChart.on('customMouseOut', callbackSpy);
        firstBar.dispatch('mouseout');
        actual = callbackSpy.calls.count();

        expect(actual).toEqual(expected);
    });

    it('should trigger the callback with the data entry as argument', () => {
        const expected = data[0];
        const firstBar = container.selectAll('.bar:nth-child(1)');
        const callbackSpy = jasmine.createSpy('callback');
        let actual;

        barChart.on('customMouseOut', callbackSpy);
        firstBar.dispatch('mouseout');
        actual = callbackSpy.calls.first().args[0];

        expect(actual).toEqual(expected);
    });
});

describe('when clicking a bar', () => {
    it('should trigger a callback once on mouse click', () => {
        const expected = 1;
        const firstBar = container.selectAll('.bar:nth-child(1)');
```

```
        const callbackSpy = jasmine.createSpy('callback');
        let actual;

        barChart.on('customMouseClick', callbackSpy);
        firstBar.dispatch('click');
        actual = callbackSpy.calls.count();

        expect(actual).toEqual(expected);
    });

    it('should trigger the callback with the data entry as argument', () => {
        const expected = data[0];
        const firstBar = container.selectAll('.bar:nth-child(1)');
        const callbackSpy = jasmine.createSpy('callback');
        let actual;

        barChart.on('customMouseClick', callbackSpy);
        firstBar.dispatch('click');
        actual = callbackSpy.calls.first().args[0];

        expect(actual).toEqual(expected);
    });
});
```

As you see, they are almost equal. In Listing 9-20, we see the code modifications that make these tests pass.

Listing 9-20. Code for the rest of events

```
//...
const dispatcher = d3.dispatch('customMouseOver', 'customMouseMove',
'customMouseOut', 'customMouseClick');
//...
// Enter
bars.enter()
  .append('rect')
    .classed('bar', true)
    .attr('x', ({letter}) => xScale(letter))
    .attr('y', ({frequency}) => yScale(frequency))
```

```
.attr('width', xScale.bandwidth())
.attr('height', ({frequency}) => chartHeight - yScale(frequency))
.on('mouseover', function(d) {
    dispatcher.call('customMouseOver', this, d);
})
.on('mousemove', function(d) {
    dispatcher.call('customMouseMove', this, d);
})
.on('mouseout', function(d) {
    dispatcher.call('customMouseOut', this, d);
})
.on('click', function(d) {
    dispatcher.call('customMouseClick', this, d);
});
```

Notice how we need to remember to add the new custom events to the declaration of the dispatch object. Another detail to note is that the value of "this" inside the event handler corresponds to the DOM element. Hence, if we want to pass the element so our users can apply styling on it, we need to pass it on the list of arguments after "d".

With the last code snippet, we have finished adding tests to our bar chart. You can see the finalized code for this section in the "step-3-events" branch of the demo repository (`http://bit.ly/pro-d3-testing-3`).

Testing the API

We saw how to test and create events for our Reusable API components. In that process, we produced the "on" getter and setter functions. We also want to test those functions. In this section, we go over the creation of tests for the accessors, both for simple and more complex accessors.

Testing Simple Accessors

We are going to start our tests as we did the "Render" and "Lifecycle" tests, with an "API" describe clause. Within the describe, we begin by adding a test to check for a chart "height" accessor. See that test in Listing 9-21.

Listing 9-21. Test for the height accessor

```
describe('API', () => {
    beforeEach(() => {
        barChart = bar();
        container = d3.select('.container');

        container.datum(data).call(barChart);
    });

    afterEach(() => {
        container.remove();
    });

    it('should provide height getter and setter', () => {
        const previous = barChart.height();
        const expected = 300;
        let actual;

        barChart.height(expected);
        actual = barChart.height();

        expect(previous).not.toEqual(actual);
        expect(actual).toEqual(expected);
    });
});
```

This code saves the default height of the chart (500 in our chart example), applies a new one (300), and gets the height again. In the assertions, we make sure that the new applied height is not the default but the expected value. As we haven't added the code in Listing 9-22 yet, this test fails.

Listing 9-22. Code for the height accessor

```
exports.height = function(_x) {
    if (!arguments.length) {
        return height;
    }
    height = _x;

    return this;
};
```

After including this code, which we talked about in Chapters 4 and 5, our tests are back to green. Let's also add a new test for the custom event getter/setter we added in the previous section. See the test in Listing 9-23.

Listing 9-23. Test for the "on" accessor

```
it('should provide a event "on" getter and setter', () => {
    const callback = () => {};
    const expected = callback;
    let actual;

    barChart.on('customMouseClick', callback);
    actual = barChart.on('customMouseClick');

    expect(actual).toEqual(expected);
});
```

This test passes, as we already added the code for the "on" accessor in the previous section.

Testing a Complex Accessor

The case of the margin accessor is a bit different, as we allow for a partial application of some of the properties of the margin object. In Listing 9-24, we show the describe clause of the test for this accessor.

Listing 9-24. Testing the margin object accessor

```
describe('margin', () => {
    it('should provide margin getter and setter', () => {
        const previous = barChart.margin();
        const expected = {top: 4, right: 4, bottom: 4, left: 4};
        let actual;

        barChart.margin(expected);
        actual = barChart.margin();

        expect(previous).not.toEqual(actual);
        expect(actual).toEqual(expected);
    });
```

```
    describe('when margins are set partially', () => {
        it('should override the default values', () => {
            const previous = barChart.margin();
            const expected = {
                ...previous,
                top: 10,
                right: 20
            };
            let actual;

            barChart.margin({
                top: 10,
                right: 20
            });
            actual = barChart.margin();

            expect(previous).not.toEqual(actual);
            expect(actual).toEqual(expected);
        })
    });
});
```

See how the first test is similar to the height test, while the one within the next describe checks for the application of the top and right properties. In Listing 9-25, we can see the code that makes these tests pass.

Listing 9-25. Code for the margin accessor

```
exports.margin = function(_x) {
    if (!arguments.length) {
        return margin;
    }
    margin = {
        ...margin,
        ..._x
    };

    return this;
};
```

150

So, with this test, we end this API testing section. You can check the code for it on the "step-4-api" branch of our demo repository (`http://bit.ly/pro-d3-testing-4`).

At the end of this chapter, and after adding tests for the rest of our API accessors, we got to a 100% test coverage, as shown in the coverage report in Listing 9-26.

Listing 9-26. Code coverage summary

```
Executed 23 of 23 SUCCESS (0.319 secs / 0.264 secs)

============================== Coverage summary ===========================
Statements    : 100% ( 60/60 )
Branches      : 100% ( 10/10 )
Functions     : 100% ( 22/22 )
Lines         : 100% ( 58/58 )
===========================================================================
✿  Done in 8.03s.
```

Summary

In this chapter, we have seen how to set up a development environment to build a chart in a Test-Driven Development way. We learned how to set up our tests using Karmatic and Jasmine. We saw the different kinds of tests we need to create to test a Reusable API component: rendering, lifecycle, and API tests. We re-created our bar chart test by test, making our tests fail before creating the code that makes them pass.

In the next chapter, we will dive deeper into build systems using Webpack and Babel. We will set our library up so we can create a distributable version and publish it into the NPM registry.

CHAPTER 10

Building Your Library

In previous chapters, we saw how to create modular, composable, and testable charts using the Reusable API. We demonstrated how that works out for Britecharts and how we can combine its components to create complex data visualizations. We also saw how to test our D3.js charts, creating professional components.

Assuming we followed these steps and have a set of chart components, we face the need for packaging them to distribute our chart library. We want to do it:

- In a performant way (bundled and minified)

- Enabling debugging and providing a great developer experience (source maps, live reload)

- Supporting old and new browsers (transforming ES2015+ into ES5 code)

- In a discoverable and standard way (using npm and diverse module formats)

Even these are numerous, they are pretty standard requirements for libraries nowadays. How can we do all of it? In this chapter, we see how to use Babel to transpile ES2015+ code, Webpack to bundle the library, and npm to distribute our work.

We'll transform our chart modules into a professional-grade library. That means we will build a project that

- Users can use in several browsers

- Maintainers and contributors enjoy working with

- Developers can download and install in various standard ways

We will learn how to use Webpack, Babel, and npm to achieve these objectives. We will see how to configure Webpack and create a professional npm module to distribute all over the world.

© Marcos Iglesias 2019
M. Iglesias, *Pro D3.js*, https://doi.org/10.1007/978-1-4842-5203-1_10

Bundling Our Library with Webpack

After the last chapters, we control some components written as ES2015 modules. Even if this format is a standard now, it is still not supported in web browsers, so our library users won't be able to use our charts directly. We need to transform these ES modules into others that can be consumed by browsers, and Webpack helps us with it.

Webpack is a module bundler for client-side JavaScript applications. In a nutshell, Webpack takes a set of entry modules and dependencies (input) and generates a file or set of files (output) which can be used by web browsers.

Webpack got popular around 2014, and although it is not the only bundler out there, it is the more popular among JavaScript developers. Webpack is a project that runs in Node.js and supports ES2015, CommonJS, and AMD modules as entry modules. It creates an output supported by web browsers that are ES5 compliant, although we can make the bundles work for older browsers too.

In this section, we learn how to install and configure Webpack. We see how to create a production bundle to distribute our library, a development configuration, and we show how to set up our test runner.

Before installing Webpack and moving forward with the rest of this chapter, we need to create our library folder and a "package.json" file. We see why we need this file in the last section. There is a wizard we can follow to create a package.json. For that, we open a new terminal window, create our library folder with "mkdir pro-d3-building", access it with "cd pro-d3-building", and run "npm init". When running the package.json wizard, we follow the prompts, filling information or accepting the defaults, as in Listing 10-1.

Listing 10-1. Running npm init in our demo project

```
$ npm init
//...

Press ^C at any time to quit.
package name: (pro-d3-building)
version: (1.0.0)
description: Demo package for the package building chapter on Pro D3.js
entry point: (index.js)
test command: yarn test
git repository: (https://github.com/Golodhros/pro-d3-building.git)
keywords: d3.js, build, package, npm
```

```
author: Marcos Iglesias Valle
license: (ISC)
About to write to /Users/miglesias/Sites/a-d3/pro-d3-building/package.json:

{
  "name": "pro-d3-building",
  "version": "1.0.0",
  "description": "Demo package for the package building chapter on Pro D3.js",
  "main": "index.js",
  "scripts": {
    "test": "yarn test"
  },
  "repository": {
    "type": "git",
    "url": "git+https://github.com/Golodhros/pro-d3-building.git"
  },
  "keywords": [
    "d3.js",
    "build",
    "package",
    "npm"
  ],
  "author": "Marcos Iglesias Valle",
  "license": "ISC",
  "bugs": {
    "url": "https://github.com/Golodhros/pro-d3-building/issues"
  },
  "homepage": "https://github.com/Golodhros/pro-d3-building#readme"
}

Is this OK? (yes)
```

After hitting enter on the last confirmation prompt, we get a package.json file that corresponds to the previewed contents. Alternatively, we could copy and paste an existing package.json and update its contents. Now we can continue with our Webpack configuration.

Installing and Configuring Webpack

In the background, Webpack analyzes the input and creates a map of its dependencies and how they relate (dependency graph). Webpack evaluates each entry module using loaders. These contain a "test" regular expression and a "use" loader value so that Webpack knows what to do with each module type. Webpack can also use plugins to execute extra logic when loading the modules.

After processing each module, Webpack injects it into the output bundle. This output bundle contains a manifest that tells browsers how to consume it. Its format depends on the build target we choose in the Webpack configuration.

To install Webpack, assuming we have the latest Node.js in our machine, we can run "npm install --save-dev webpack webpack-cli" or "yarn add -D webpack webpack-cli". Then, we add to our package.json file the scripts object in Listing 10-2.

Listing 10-2. The initial scripts object in our package.json

```
"scripts": {
  "test": "yarn test",
  "build": "webpack --config webpack.config.js"
},
```

This script runs Webpack using "webpack-cli" using the configuration in the "webpack.config.js" file we create. This file contains the setup needed to configure the different elements of a Webpack bundling pipeline, elements that we review now.

Entry

The "entry" property specifies where we start to build our project dependency graph. Webpack takes it from there and figures out which other modules are necessary to create the bundle.

Output

The "output" object of the configuration tells Webpack where to place the resulting bundle and how to call it. Within "output," we specify the "filename" and destination "path." We can also use "[name]" to create multiple bundles using the entries' filenames. For example, if we have "file1.js" and "file2.js" as entries, we could get "file1.min.js" and "file2.min.js" as outputs.

Loaders

Webpack loaders allow us to handle all kind of assets, not only JavaScript and JSON files. Loaders convert files into valid modules, so they can be added to the dependency graph and, ultimately, to the output bundle. We define for each module the "rules" property to list the loaders. See an example in Listing 10-3.

Listing 10-3. A CSS loader example

```
module: {
    rules: [
        {
            test:/\.scss$/,
            use: [
                'style-loader',
                'css-loader',
            ],
            exclude: /node_modules/,
        },
    ],
},
```

Each loader has a "test" and "use" properties, defining the types of files to transform and which loader takes care of them. We also employ an "exclude" property to avoid processing unnecessary modules.

Plugins

Plugins enable doing different tasks while processing the entry modules. Webpack uses the plugins we declare when it finishes a bundle. Listing 10-4 shows an example of plugin declarations.

Listing 10-4. Adding plugins to the bundling pipeline

```
plugins: [
    new DashboardPlugin(),
    new BundleAnalyzerPlugin({
        analyzerPort: 123
    }),
],
```

To use the plugins property array, we first require the plugins at the top of the file and then instantiate the plugins using the "new" operator.

Mode

Since Webpack 4, we should set the "mode" configuration property to "development," "production," or "none." This value activates Webpack's default optimizations for the different development modes, making it easier for maintainers to use convenient plugin defaults.

Creating a Production Bundle

We covered the components of a Webpack configuration file, and now we are ready to tackle the configuration for our library's production bundle. We want to create a library that allows getting imported as an ES2015 module, CommonJS, AMD module, and global by loading a script tag. To simplify matters, we are going to produce a single output that bundles all our charts together.

We are going to call our library "pro-d3-building", so it matches the repository for this chapter. In Listing 10-5, we can see the contents of the "webpack.config.js" file.

Listing 10-5. Production bundle Webpack configuration

```
const path = require('path');
const merge = require('webpack-merge');

const parts = require('./webpack.parts');
const constants = require('./webpack.constants');

const prodBundleConfig = merge([
    {
        mode: 'production',
        devtool: 'source-map',
        entry: {
            proD3Building: constants.PATHS.bundleIndex
        },
```

```
        output: {
            path: path.resolve(__dirname, 'dist/'),
            filename: 'proD3Building.min.js',
            library: ['proD3Building'],
            libraryTarget: 'umd'
        },
    },
    parts.babelLoader(),
    parts.cssLoader(),
    parts.externals(),
]);

module.exports = (env) => {
    if (env === 'production') {
        return prodBundleConfig;
    }
};
```

In the first lines of our Webpack configuration, we import the node "path" library to help us find files in the system. We also require "webpack-merge" (http://bit. ly/pro-d3-webpack-merge), a utility library to concatenate configuration objects. WebpackMerge allows us to split our Webpack configuration into small objects. These can be reused and composed among the configuration pipelines we create. We should install it by running "yarn add -D webpack-merge".

Then, we load the "webpack.parts.js" and "webpack.constants.js" files that we create and leave empty. The former file contains the Webpack configuration objects we are going to compose, while the latter contains shared constants such as paths and lists of charts.

The "prodBundleConfig" object is where our production configuration lives, and we use the "merge" function from "webpack-merge" to compose the shared parts with the specifics of the production setup. Here we specify

- **mode**: We use the "production" default setup that activates features like minification with Terser and concatenation of modules.

- **devtool**: We choose the slow but accurate "source-map" devtool, so we can provide our users with good source maps to our chart's code.

- **entry**: We start the bundling process from the index file we show in Listing 10-5.

- **output**: We provide the output bundle configuration, specifically

  - **path**: Where Webpack is going to place the resulting bundle.

  - **filename**: The name of the bundle file.

  - **library**: The resulting global object name (window. proD3Building) when we load the library with a script tag.

  - **libraryTarget**: The format of the library. "UMD" is a widely compatible module system that allows its use as a CommonJS and AMD module.

- **babelLoader**: A custom configuration object that we describe in the section dedicated to Babel in this chapter.

- **cssLoader**: A configuration object to load the stylesheets of our charts.

- **externals**: An object specifying the external libraries we load. In our case, it contains only D3.js.

Finally, we export a function that returns different bundle pipelines depending on an environment variable that can be "development," "production," or "test." We set the variable as an argument in our npm script call, such as "'build": "webpack --config webpack.config.js --env=production"'.

In the entry file of our configuration (src/index.js), we need to load all the components of our library, as noted in Listing 10-6.

Listing 10-6. Index file

```
export {default as bar} from './charts/barChart.js';
```

See how we export and import all at once, using the ES module notation. We need to bring the bar chart code and its styles from Chapter 9 along with its tests and place them in the "/src/charts" folder.

We also install D3.js by running "yarn add -P d3" to add it as a peer dependency. This means that our library depends on the user having D3.js installed. The way we tell Webpack about it so that D3.js doesn't get added to the output is by using the "external" property. See how we set it within the parts file in Listing 10-7.

Listing 10-7. File webpack.parts.js with externals and cssLoader

```
exports.externals = () => ({
    externals: {
        commonjs: 'd3',
        amd: 'd3',
        root: 'd3'
    },
});

// Loaders
exports.cssLoader = () => ({
    module: {
        rules: [
            {
                test: /\.css$/,
                use: [
                    'style-loader',
                    'css-loader',
                ]
            },
        ],
    },
});
exports.babelLoader = () => ({});
```

Notice how we added the external for CommonJS, AMD, and root modules, as this is necessary for UMD outputs like the one we specified in our "libraryTarget" property. Our cssLoader object follows the Webpack documentation, using the "style-loader" and "css-loader" when processing ".css" files. We install those by running "yarn add -D style-loader css-loader".

At this point, and after adding the index path to the constants file, we would be able to run "yarn build" and get the output in Listing 10-8.

Listing 10-8. Our first run log of "yarn build"

```
$ yarn build
yarn run v1.16.0
$ webpack --config webpack.config.js --env=production
Hash: 5977d9e3a04ecd337815
Version: webpack 4.35.2
Time: 5256ms
Built at: 07/07/2019 2:18:20 PM
                    Asset      Size  Chunks            Chunk Names
    proD3Building.min.js  137 KiB       0  [emitted]   proD3Building
proD3Building.min.js.map  617 KiB       0  [emitted]   proD3Building
Entrypoint proD3Building = proD3Building.min.js proD3Building.min.js.map
[0] ./src/charts/barChart.css 1.08 KiB {0} [built]
[1] ./node_modules/css-loader/dist/cjs.js!./src/charts/barChart.css 292
bytes {0} [built]
[5] ./src/index.js + 517 modules 536 KiB {0} [built]
    | ./src/index.js 53 bytes [built]
    | ./src/charts/barChart.js 4.4 KiB [built]
    |     + 516 hidden modules
    + 3 hidden modules
✨   Done in 6.99s.
```

This process results in Webpack creating two files within the "/dist" folder. One is
our bundled chart (proD3Building.min.js) and the other its source map (proD3Building.
min.js.map). We need to update the "main" property in our package.json file to point to
the former, so it looks like this: "'main": "/dist/proD3Building.min.js'". That way, when
somebody imports our published npm module, they will use the minified bundle as the
default entry when requiring the "pro-d3-building" library.

One last step before committing this code to our repository is to add a ".gitignore"
file listing the elements we don't want to upload. You can check this file and the rest of
logic at this point by examining the "step-1-production-build" branch of the repository
(http://bit.ly/pro-d3-building-step-1).

The Development Setup

If we open the minified bundle we created in the previous section, we see a single line of JavaScript that starts with some module-related gibberish and continues with obfuscated code. This content doesn't help us make sure we obtained the desired output. Also, to test it manually, we would need to copy/paste this file and use it somewhere else. Not ideal. We need a development setup so that maintainers can check if the current code works and to experiment with new features before sharing them with the community.

Webpack has two interfaces. One is the "webpack-cli" module we installed at the beginning and ran in our build script. The other is the "webpack-dev-server" tool, which we install by running "yarn add -D webpack-dev-server".

Webpack-dev-server is an Express (https://expressjs.com/) Node.js server that calls Webpack internally. It provides extra functionality when developing apps or libraries, such as

- Watch mode (--watch), which keeps track of the changes in our files.

- Live reload (--inline), which provides automatic refreshes when our source code files change.

- Hot Module Replacement (--hot). Similar to the previous, it also keeps the state of the application when updating it with the new changes.

To configure the previous options, we can set them as inline arguments when calling "webpack-dev-server" or we can use a "devServer" object in our Webpack configuration. In Listing 10-9, we can see the development configuration we use for our "proD3Building" library.

Listing 10-9. Development configuration

```
const path = require('path');
const merge = require('webpack-merge');

const HtmlWebpackPlugin = require('html-webpack-plugin');

const parts = require('./webpack.parts');
const constants = require('./webpack.constants');

//... Production Configuration
```

```
const devConfig = merge([
    {
        mode: 'development',
        devtool: 'cheap-eval-source-map',
        entry: constants.DEMOS,
        output: {
            path: path.resolve(__dirname, 'demos/build'),
            filename: '[name].js'
        },
        devServer: {
            contentBase: './demos/build',
            port: 8001,
            inline: true,
            hot: true,
            open: true,
        },
        plugins: [
            new HtmlWebpackPlugin({
                title: 'Development',
                template: 'src/demos/index.html'
            })
        ],
    },
    parts.cssLoader(),
    parts.babelLoader(),
]);

module.exports = (env) => {

    if (env === 'dev') {
        return devConfig;
    }

    if (env === 'production') {
        return prodBundleConfig;
    }
};
```

Let's analyze this configuration. We start by setting the mode to "development," to name our modules using the "NamedModulesPlugin". Then, we set the "devtool" option to "cheap-eval-source-map", which trades a worse accuracy for a faster bundling time on the source map generation process.

As the entry of this bundle, we are going to use a demo file that loads our chart. We use the "src/index.js" file from the previous chapter, along with a simple HTML template file we store in the "src/demos" folder. We use the "HtmlWebpackPlugin" that we install by running "yarn add -D html-webpack-plugin" and add it to the plugins array. Webpack takes the HTML template and extends it with the modules generated in the pipeline.

We build our output inside the "demos/build" folder, although "webpack-dev-server" won't create any file when running in "inline" mode. We also keep the demo file name by setting filename to "[name].js".

In the devServer object, we specify the inline and hot configurations for "webpack-dev-server". We add the port we are going to use in our Express server to show the demo and activate the "open" flag to initiate a browser tab when Webpack finishes the build. We need to install D3.js as a development dependency, running "yarn add -D d3" so that we can get our demo working.

We are reusing the "cssLoader" and the "babelLoader" object we talk about later in the chapter. The "merge" function includes both in the development configuration.

Lastly, we add a new if statement on our exported function, checking for the "dev" environment variable to run this new bundling pipeline. Now, we only need to add this line to our npm scripts: "'dev": "webpack-dev-server --env=dev",' and run "yarn dev" to be able to see something like Figure 10-1.

Bar Chart

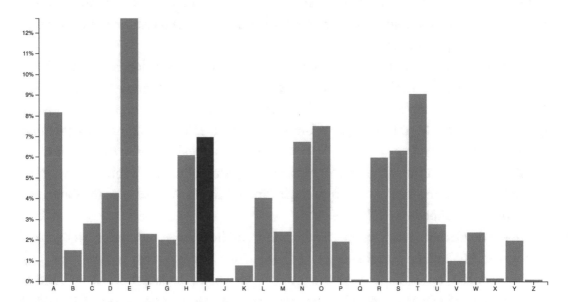

Figure 10-1. *Our bar chart demo*

This bar chart demo allows us to test our chart manually and with real data, supplying us a playground to test our components and try new features. You can access the code at this point in the "step-2-dev-build" branch of this chapter's repository (`http://bit.ly/pro-d3-building-step-2`).

Running Our Tests

In the previous section, we got to see our library's unique chart rendering on a page. This demo allows for manual testing of our charts. However, that's not enough for a professional charting library. We want to have automated testing working as well, the same way we got it in Chapter 9. In this section, we see what we need to do to have Karma running and working with our Webpack pipeline.

First of all, we install the dependencies to set up the Karma test runner along Webpack. They are

- **karma**: The core library of the Karma project

- **karma-webpack**: A plugin to use Karma along with Webpack

- **karma-jasmine**: The plugin that enables the use of Jasmine to write our tests

- **karma-sourcemap-loader**: A plugin to load our source maps when debugging our tests in the browser

- **karma-chrome-launcher**: Allows us to trigger our tests in a Google Chrome web browser.

As usual, we install all these dependencies using Yarn by running

```
'yarn add -D karma karma-webpack karma-sourcemap-loader karma-chrome-
launcher karma-jasmine'.
```

Now we need to configure Karma, and for it, we follow its wizard in the command line by running "karma init". This command presents a series of prompts. In them, we select Jasmine as our test framework, avoid using Require.js, select Chrome as the browser, and indicate "src/tests.webpack.js" as the source of our tests. We can think of "tests.webpack. js" as the "index.js" file for our tests, and it looks like the code in Listing 10-10.

Listing 10-10. The tests.webpack.js file

```
const context = require.context('./charts', true, /\.test\.js$/);

context.keys().forEach(context);
```

This code creates a context for all tests in the "charts" folder and, for each file, calls the context function that requires the files and loads them. Next, we move into our Webpack configuration file and create a new configuration that maps to the "test" environment variable. It looks like the code in Listing 10-11.

Listing 10-11. The test configuration

```
//... Dependencies imports
//... Production and Development configurations

const testConfig = merge([
    {
        mode: 'development',
        devtool: 'inline-source-map',
        resolve: {
```

```
            modules: [
                path.resolve(__dirname, 'src/charts'),
                'node_modules',
            ],
        },
    },
    parts.cssLoader(),
    parts.babelLoader(),
]);

module.exports = (env) => {
    if (env === 'dev') {
        return devConfig;
    }
    if (env === 'test') {
        return testConfig;
    }
    if (env === 'production') {
        return prodBundleConfig;
    }
};
```

The particular thing about this configuration is that it doesn't need an entry or an output property. That's because we specify the entry in the Karma configuration file, which you can see in Listing 10-12.

Listing 10-12. The karma.conf.js file

```
// Karma configuration
const webpack = require('webpack');
const webpackConfig = require('./webpack.config');

module.exports = function(config) {
  config.set({

    // base path that will be used to resolve all patterns (eg. files,
    exclude)
    basePath: ",
```

```
// frameworks to use
// available frameworks: https://npmjs.org/browse/keyword/karma-adapter
frameworks: ['jasmine'],

// list of files / patterns to load in the browser
files: [
    'src/tests.webpack.js'
],

// preprocess matching files before serving them to the browser
// available preprocessors: https://npmjs.org/browse/keyword/karma-
preprocessor
preprocessors: {
    'src/tests.webpack.js': [ 'webpack', 'sourcemap' ]
},

webpack: webpackConfig('test'),

//... Code ommitted for brevity
  })
}
```

In this configuration file, we specify our test framework (Jasmine) and point Karma to our test entry point ("src/tests.webpack.js"). On that entry point, we ask Karma to run the Webpack and Sourcemap plugins before processing the files with our Webpack test configuration.

Now, we only need to update the test script command in our package.json to read: "'test": "karma start --env=test",'. Running "yarn test" produces the terminal log in Listing 10-13.

Listing 10-13. Our tests running

```
$ yarn test
yarn run v1.16.0
$ karma start --env=test
// ...
07 07 2019 20:48:17.068:WARN [karma]: No captured browser, open http://
localhost:9876/
```

```
07 07 2019 20:48:17.075:INFO [karma-server]: Karma v4.1.0 server started at
http://0.0.0.0:9876/
07 07 2019 20:48:17.076:INFO [launcher]: Launching browsers Chrome with
concurrency unlimited
07 07 2019 20:48:17.091:INFO [launcher]: Starting browser Chrome
07 07 2019 20:48:18.692:INFO [Chrome 75.0.3770 (Mac OS X 10.12.6)]:
Connected on socket RXE75EE2UAkJ98GwAAAA with id 94795783
. . . . . . . . . . . . . . . . . . . . .
Chrome 75.0.3770 (Mac OS X 10.12.6): Executed 23 of 23 SUCCESS (0.164 secs
/ 0.124 secs)
```

Also, they are green and passing! When testing our logic, we want to have a measure to describe how well tested it is. This measure is the test coverage of our code, and we can add it by using Istanbul. For that, we need to create a new loader in the webpack. parts.js file. It looks like the code in Listing 10-14.

Listing 10-14. The Istanbul code coverage loader

```javascript
exports.istanbulLoader = () => ({
    module: {
        rules: [
            {
                test: /\.js?$/,
                include: /src/,
                exclude: /(node_modules|tests.webpack.js)/,
                use: [{
                    loader: 'istanbul-instrumenter-loader',
                    query: {
                        esModules: true
                    }
                }],
            }
        ]
    }
});
```

This loader requires a new package that we install along with the coverage plugin for Karma by running "yarn add -D istanbul-instrumenter-loader karma-coverage". On the Karma configuration, we update the reporters to add a "coverage" item and the preprocessors by adding this line: "'src/charts/*.js': ["coverage"]", as well as the whole block for the "coverageReporter" key you can check in the repository (http://bit.ly/pro-d3-coverage-setup).

The command-line results after running "yarn test" look like the log in Listing 10-15.

Listing 10-15. Code coverage report in the command line

```
.....................
Chrome 75.0.3770 (Mac OS X 10.12.6): Executed 23 of 23 SUCCESS (0.155 secs /
0.121 secs)
-------------------|----------|----------|----------|----------|----------------|
File               | % Stmts  | % Branch | % Funcs  | % Lines  |Uncovered Lines |
-------------------|----------|----------|----------|----------|----------------|
 charts/           |      100 |      100 |    98.51 |      100 |                |
  barChart.js      |      100 |      100 |      100 |      100 |                |
  barChart.test.js |      100 |      100 |    97.78 |      100 |                |
-------------------|----------|----------|----------|----------|----------------|
All files          |      100 |      100 |    98.51 |      100 |                |
-------------------|----------|----------|----------|----------|----------------|
```

That's a pretty good coverage level, but it isn't that hard when we are testing only one file! You can check the completed code of this section in the "step-3-tests-running" branch of this chapter's repository (http://bit.ly/pro-d3-building-step-3).

Another step that I highly encourage to do is to set up a continuous integration (CI) tool to run the tests. Due to lack of space, we can't go over it here, but you can check the Karma documentation (http://bit.ly/pro-d3-building-karma-travis). The only caveat is that the CI tools support for browsers are limited, so maybe you end up using Firefox or PhantomJS instead of Chrome when testing on the CI.

Using Babel to Transpile Our Code

When developing for the Web, not all web browsers support the different JavaScript features (http://bit.ly/pro-d3-es6-compatibility). In this chapter, we have created a bundle that contains ES2015+ features that can be run by modern browsers.

However, users who employ older browsers won't be able to consume our charts. There could be many reasons for them to use these browsers, and we shouldn't judge them for it, so we want to make sure we empower them to use our library.

The prevailing solution to avoid compatibility issues is to use Babel (`https://babeljs.io/`). From their documentation, here is the definition of the project: "Babel is a toolchain that is mainly used to convert ECMAScript 2015+ code into a backward-compatible version of JavaScript in current and older browsers or environments."

Babel is what is called a "code transpiler." That is a set of functions that allows us to compile modern JavaScript code into a version of JavaScript that is compatible with more web browsers (or older Node.js versions). With Babel we can also

- Transform syntax in our library

- Polyfill features missing in our target browsers

- Transform codebases using codemods, scripts that help to automate code refactors

- Transpile TypeScript, stripping out annotations

In this section, we explore how does Babel work, how can we install it, and some configuration basics. We learn how to use Babel in our Webpack pipeline, making our charts available to a full range of web browsers.

Babel Fundamentals

Babel is based on a plugin ecosystem that allows us to compose transformation pipelines. A Babel plugin is a JavaScript function that tells Babel how to run code transformations. There are many plugins, each one dealing with a specific ES2015+ feature. This multiplicity can be problematic, as we need to keep track of the features we are using and add or remove Babel plugins accordingly. However, Babel provides a solution to make plugins easy to use: Babel presets.

Babel presets help us to avoid adding feature support one by one. We provide Babel with a list of browsers, and the "env" preset figures out the plugins necessary to assist those web browsers. We can create a list of browsers (`http://bit.ly/pro-d3-browserlist`) in several formats, such as .browserslistrc file, or directly within our package.json. This browser list is a standard that can be used by other projects such as PostCSS, ESLint, and Autoprefixer. When creating a browser list, we provide a "browser query" that specifies the web browser support. To review this list, we can use `https://browserl.ist/`, to see if our query creates a browser list that makes sense.

We can see an example of this setup using our library. Let's assume we want to support all modern browsers, but we have a particular requirement to handle Internet Explorer 10. We check the documentation and reach to this query: "defaults, IE 10", which we can add to our package.json with "'browserslist': "defaults, IE 10".

Next, we need to create the configuration for Babel (`http://bit.ly/pro-d3-babel-conf`). We can write it in various places, and for consistency, we use the package.json as noted in Listing 10-16.

Listing 10-16. Our babel configuration in package.json

```
//...
"browserslist": "defaults, IE 10",
"babel": {
    "presets": [
            ["@babel/preset-env", {
                    "debug":true
            }]
    ]
}
```

Note how we are setting the debug flag to "true"; this option shows the plugins used and their version in the terminal. You can see the rest of the options of the "env" preset in the documentation (`http://bit.ly/pro-d3-babel-preset-env`).

Using Babel with Webpack

We just set up the Babel configuration, and we have our project ready to be transpiled. Now we need to run Babel with our Webpack pipeline, as we describe in this section.

First, we install the different features that live in different packages within the Babel repository. Here are the packages we need:

- **@babel/core**: The core Babel package, responsible for the transpilation process

- **@babel/preset-env**: The "env" preset package, which applies to our JavaScript output the support level given our browser list

- **babel-loader**: A Webpack loader to transpile code using Babel

We use Yarn to add this to our project by running "yarn add -D @babel/core @babel/preset-env babel-loader". Note how we use the "-D" flag of Yarn, which adds these packages as development dependencies.

Now we are ready to create a new loader object that uses Babel to transpile all our JavaScript files using our Babel configuration. In Listing 10-17, we can see the object we add to our webpack.parts.js file.

Listing 10-17. Babel loader in webpack.parts.js

```
exports.babelLoader = () => ({
    module: {
        rules: [
            {
                test: /\.js$/,
                exclude: /node_modules/,
                use: ['babel-loader'],
            },
        ],
    },
});
```

Notice how we define the "module" object again, which would be an error if we weren't using "webpack-merge" to apply this configuration. As we have included this loader in our pipelines, we don't need to do anything else. Now, every time we run "yarn build," "yarn dev," or "yarn test" in the command line, we can read a command-line log listing the plugins used by Babel.

To test that our charts work using the previous code, we need to run our demos with an Internet Explorer 10 browser. For that, we could use a browser testing service like BrowserStack (https://browserstack.com/) and Sauce Labs (https://saucelabs.com/) or download a virtual machine from Microsoft's web site (http://bit.ly/pro-d3-windows-vms). As earlier, you can find the finalized code for this step in the "step-4-babel-transpiling" branch of the repo (http://bit.ly/pro-d3-building-step-4).

Publishing Packages with npm

We have seen how we can create a library bundle that puts together all our charts into a single file. We also described how to use Babel to make this JavaScript bundle compatible with a wide range of web browsers. Now we want to share our library, managing its version and also its dependencies. We want to allow the community of JavaScript developers to use our library too. The best way to distribute this work is by using the npm registry to make our library public.

In this section, we introduce the npm package registry and the "package.json" file that describes its packages. We show how we can publish our library into the registry and update it with the latest version.

Introducing npm and the package.json File

npm (`www.npmjs.com/`) is JavaScript's primary package registry, and thanks to the rising popularity of JavaScript, it is also the largest code package collection in the world. npm is distributed with Node.js, and it is free for sharing packages publicly, making it ideal for open source software (OSS) distribution.

The npm registry is a database of JavaScript packages where code and metadata about that code forms each package. Thus, an npm package is a file or a directory (the code) described by a package.json file (the metadata). It can come in different formats, from a compressed tarball to a simple URL pointing to the package. Packages usually contain a module that can be loaded by Node.js require function.

However, npm isn't only a web registry for open source used by developers to share code. npm features a command-line interface (CLI) that allows us to manage our libraries and applications, even if we don't plan to publish them on the registry.

We do this by using the "package.json" file, which is a file where we give context about the package or application. The primary package.json properties are

- **name**: States the name for the package (required).

- **version**: The current version number in format x.x.x (required).

- **description**: A short description that helps people discover the package.

- **author**: Name, email, and web site of the author.

- **contributors**: An array of people that contributed to the project.

- **main**: The path for the main entry point of the package when required by other applications ("index.js" is the default).

- **module**: Specifies the ES module entry point for bundlers.

- **keywords**: List of words that helps to make the package discoverable.

- **homepage**: The URL of the project's homepage.

- **license**: The license type, so people know if they can use the project. We can see the different identifiers in `https://spdx.org/licenses/`.

- **scripts**: A dictionary containing a list of script commands, where the key is the event and the value the command to run at that point.

- **dependencies**: A list of the dependencies the package needs to work, along with their versions or their specific location.

- **devDependencies**: Lists the dependencies that are not necessary for running the package, but required to develop on it.

- **peerDependencies**: Specifies the compatibility of the package with other libraries.

There are a bunch more of properties, and we can consult the whole list in npm's documentation (`http://bit.ly/pro-d3-package-conf`). The package.json file makes it easy to manage and install a package. It includes the version of the package and the list of the project dependencies, and it makes the project output reproducible, allowing developers to work together on the same project.

Adding Our Package to the npm Registry

Now that we learned what the npm registry is and what to include in our "package.json" file, let's see the steps to publish our library. To contribute packages to the npm registry, we need to follow this process:

1. Create an npm user account. npm makes this step easy, as the CLI tool includes a command that prompts us with some questions and creates an account from our terminal window. We run "npm adduser" and fill our username, password, and email to get us signed in.

2. Create a package.json file. In this chapter, we created and filled "package.json" file that contains all the information we need.

3. Create the "main" entry point. This property makes the package available to users. We don't need to update ours, as "/dist/proD3Building.min.js" is the right entry point.

4. Add a .npmignore file. This file lists the files and folders that we want to exclude from our finished package. These are usually

    •   Test files

    •   Tooling configurations, such as Travis, Webpack, and Babel-related files.

    •   Tool or build logs

    •   Development-only information, like our contributing guide, project contributors, and similar.

In our case, it is similar to our .gitignore, but it adds the tooling configuration and avoids hiding the dist folder.

1. Write a "README.md" Markdown file. A Markdown-formatted text is a simplified way of styling text on the Web. We write here essential documentation that helps developers find your package and provides installation and usage instructions. I recommend checking "The Art of Readme" (`http://bit.ly/pro-d3-readme`) to learn about best practices for Readme files.

2. Publish the package. We use the CLI command "npm publish", getting a log similar to what we see in Listing 10-18.

Listing 10-18. `npm publish log`

```
npm publish
npm notice
npm notice 🎁  pro-d3-building@1.0.0
npm notice === Tarball Contents ===
npm notice 1.5kB    package.json
npm notice 763B     README.md
npm notice 141.3kB dist/proD3Building.min.js
npm notice 631.7kB dist/proD3Building.min.js.map
npm notice 137B     src/charts/barChart.css
npm notice 4.5kB    src/charts/barChart.js
npm notice 12.5kB   src/charts/barChart.test.js
npm notice 1.6kB    src/demos/demo-bar.js
npm notice 453B     src/demos/index.html
npm notice 53B      src/index.js
npm notice 269B     src/tests.webpack.js
npm notice === Tarball Details ===
npm notice name:          pro-d3-building
npm notice version:       1.0.0
npm notice package size:  207.7 kB
npm notice unpacked size: 794.9 kB
npm notice shasum:        30529ff408379bfafcc6c04f8484bb17c5fcfba0
npm notice integrity:     sha512-gpj5lhvMOW7BV[...]k2oJszEWwdPew==
npm notice total files:   11
npm notice
+ pro-d3-building@1.0.0
```

See how we get a list of the elements included in the package, which we can adjust by adding or removing entries in the .npmignore file. Once finished, we can test the publishing success in two ways:

- Visiting the registry's web site at `https://npmjs.com/package/<package-name>` and making sure it exists.

- In a new terminal, create a temporal folder and install our package: "mkdir tmp && cd tmp && npm install <package-name>". See how npm creates a "node_modules/" folder, and inside it, we should find our distribution files.

Feel free to see examples of the .npmignore, README.md, and package.json files in the repository (`http://bit.ly/pro-d3-building-repo`). You can also see our demo package live in `https://npmjs.com/package/pro-d3-building`, install it with "npm install pro-d3-building", and examine the contents.

Updating and Maintaining Our Library

At this point, we have a demo repository and a package published in the npm registry. That is great, but it is only the beginning. Creating and maintaining a library is hard work, especially if your goal is to create an OSS community around it. In this section, we see how we can update our library with the latest changes, learn about package versioning, and show some extra resources that help you get started in the OSS maintainer's life.

Let's assume we have improved our library and have some updates for our users. We updated our production build, maybe with a new chart, and want to make the new component available to our community. Once we are ready, we can use the "npm version" (`http://bit.ly/pro-d3-npm-version-conf`) CLI command to bump the package version.

We could also label the new commit and push it at once by running 'npm version minor -m "Upgrade to %s to provide a new chart"'. This version command updates the version in our package.json, pushing a new commit to our repository in which the symbol "%s" is swapped with the new version number. Lastly, we republish our package by running "npm publish" in the command line.

Note how we called the version command with the argument "minor". This keyword is part of semantic versioning or "semver," which is a widely accepted versioning convention among the OSS community. This convention states some rules:

- A Major version involves a change in the API that breaks with previous behavior.

- A Minor version means we have added some new features that are backward-compatible.

- A Patch version is when we fix bugs and release a backward-compatible version of the package.

Semantic versioning can be a bit confusing at the beginning, but it is critical to understand and navigate the dependencies in the JavaScript ecosystem. We can read more about it in its specification (`https://semver.org/`) and use the semver calculator tool (`https://semver.npmjs.com/`) to make sure we don't mess up our versions.

Creating an open source project can be a very casual thing for some developers while meaning a lot for others. If you are new to OSS, this guide (`https://opensource.guide/starting-a-project/`) walks you through some of the steps and considerations we don't have space to talk about in this book. The open source community is exceptionally open and welcoming, and there are lots of resources you can follow. We have podcasts (`http://bit.ly/pro-d3-oss-podcast`), open books (`https://survivejs.com/maintenance/preface/`), and publications (`http://bit.ly/pro-d3-oss-reading-list`) we can consult to help us navigate this world.

Summary

In this chapter, we have published our first open source charting library. For that, we leveraged the popular Webpack bundling library to create production, development, and test pipelines. We learned how to use Babel to make our library accessible to a broader audience of web users. On top of all that, we employed npm to publish and update our library.

In the next chapter, we are going to add the cherry on the cake by shipping an up-to-date documentation for our library.

CHAPTER 11

Creating Documentation

This chapter deals with documenting your chart library. We talk briefly about the importance of documentation and the usual challenges associated with it. We will see how we can overcome these by adding comments to our source code and generate our documentation from them.

You will learn how to document your code, generate a customized documentation page, and publish it. You will also discover ways in which you can maintain your documentation up to date and enforce other team members to follow your lead.

The Value of Documentation

All software projects benefit from having great documentation. Developers regard docs as crucial for projects, but paradoxically, docs are usually oversight. Documentation is vital for a software project because

- It holds the team's experience and knowledge of the field.

- It increases developer satisfaction.

- It helps onboarding new users and team members.

- It enables the creation of inclusive open source communities.

However, not everything is easy regarding documentation. Creating docs is usually perceived by engineers as a "boring" task. When searching for docs, some engineers get frustrated because they are scattered or poorly organized. Lastly, developers complain about out-of-date documents, which spread mistrust in the whole documentation.

© Marcos Iglesias 2019
M. Iglesias, *Pro D3.js*, https://doi.org/10.1007/978-1-4842-5203-1_11

How can we create excellent documentation for our library without falling into these issues? The strategy we suggest in this chapter is to add the documentation on the code and generate docs from it. For that, we will

1. Add annotations to our source code

2. Generate and customize documentation from these comments

3. Publish and maintain this documentation

Keep on reading to learn the steps to achieve this solution.

Commenting Our Code with JSDoc Annotations

In this chapter, we are going to follow the docs-as-code strategy (`http://bit.ly/pro-d3-docs-as-code`). Docs-as-code is an approach that aims to use software development tools to create documentation. That means we use version control, markdown files, linting, and code reviews to create and maintain the documentation of our project.

When using docs-as-code, we can employ several ways to generate our markdown files. However, the de facto standard to document JavaScript code is JSDoc annotations.

Introducing JSDoc

JSDoc is both an API documentation generator tool and a source code annotation syntax for JavaScript projects. The syntax is based on a series of tags (terms preceded by an "@" symbol) which, used before each function or module, describe their properties and purpose.

The inner workings of the generator are simple. Developers add comments to their code with the JSDoc syntax and run the JSDoc or a compatible tool. This tool scans the code and extracts the comments to generate documentation in diverse formats.

JSDoc Syntax by Example

The JSDoc syntax and semantics are like those of Javadoc, which is used for documenting Java code. In this section, we review tags organized into two groups: those for functions and those for modules. We do it using examples from our bar chart module.

Functions

When commenting functions, we can use a variety of tags (`http://bit.ly/pro-d3-js-doc-block`). Following is a selection of the most useful:

- **@param**: It is by far the most common tag. It specifies input parameters and their types. A typical @param declaration includes the "@param" tag, the type, the name, and a description of the argument. See the schema: @param { <type> } <name> <description>

- **@return**: Describes the return (if any) of the function. Its schema is similar: @return { <type> } <description>

- **@private and @public**: Placing one of these tags informs whether the function is private or public. It separates the comments for the public documentation from those that remain private.

- **@link**: We can add links to internal pages or external resources using @link. See its schema: @link {<URL> | <link text>}

Let's see in Listing 11-1 an example of an annotated private function from our bar chart.

Listing 11-1. Private function comments

```
/**
 * Builds the SVG element that will contain the chart
 * @param  {HTMLElement} container  DOM element that will work as the
   container of the graph
 * @private
 */
function buildSVG(container){
    if (!svg) {
        svg = d3.select(container)
          .append('svg')
            .classed('bar-chart', true);

        buildContainerGroups();
    }
```

```
    svg
        .attr('width', width)
        .attr('height', height);
}
```

Here is an example of a private function with an input. We use the standard HTMLElement as the type of the input argument, which we name "container" within the function. In Listing 11-2, we show a public accessor function that is part of the API.

Listing 11-2. Public accessor function comments

```
/**
 * Gets or Sets the height of the chart
 * @param  {Number} [_x=500]     Desired height for the chart
 * @return {Number | Module}     Current height or Chart module to chain calls
 * @public
 */
exports.height = function(_x) {
    if (!arguments.length) {
        return height;
    }
    height = _x;

    return this;
};
```

In this code, we declare a single optional argument called "_x", whose default value is 500. As return values, this function can return either a number or the chart module itself. Adding the @public tag means that this comment is part of the public documentation of the module.

Note how in both examples, we start our JSDoc comments with "/**". This beginning communicates that the comment is a JSDoc annotation.

Modules

When documenting modules (`http://bit.ly/pro-d3-jsdoc-modules`) or classes (`http://bit.ly/pro-d3-jsdoc-classes`), we use additional tags like

- **@module**: It creates an identifier for the module and marks the file as such. This associates all methods of the file with the module name. The schema is simple: @module <ModuleName>

- **@requires**: This tag identifies a dependency of the module. Its schema is: @requires <ModuleName>

- **@tutorial**: It creates a link to a tutorial (`http://bit.ly/pro-d3-jsdoc-tutorials`) by stating the name of its HTML page. It looks like this: @tutorial <FileName>

- **@example**: This tag shows an example of use for the module or function. The schema is the following: @example <example code>

We annotate our bar chart module using these tags, as we show in Listing 11-3.

Listing 11-3. Comments for the bar chart module

```
/**
* Bar Chart Reusable API component that renders a
* simple and configurable bar chart.
*
* @module Bar
* @tutorial bar
* @requires d3
*
* @example
* const barChart = bar();
*
* barChart
*     .height(500)
*     .width(800);
*
```

```
* d3Selection.select('.css-selector')
*       .datum(dataset)
*       .call(barChart);
*
*/
  function bar() {
    //...
}
```

Notice how we can add as many code lines as we want below an @example tag. Later in this chapter, we see how this example code looks like when we generate the documentation.

Data

We have seen how to comment on functions and modules. However, a crucial part of any charting library is the data we feed to the charts. To document the data shape, we can use a JSDoc tag that lets us define a custom type. This tag is "@typedef". We use @typedef to state the schema of the data that the chart uses. The @typedef tag is especially useful when we refer custom types on @param or @return tags.

To create a complex data object, we start by naming it with the @typedef tag. Then, below the definition, we create @property tags that name, type, and describe each of the custom type properties. We can see it better with an example such as the one in Listing 11-4.

Listing 11-4. Defining a complex data type

```
/**
 * @typedef BarData
 * @type {Object[]}
 * @property {String} letter        Name of the letter (required)
 * @property {Number} frequency     Value of its frequency (required)
 *
 * @example
 * [
 *     {
 *         letter: 'A',
 *         frequency: 0.08167
 *     },
```

```
 *      {
 *          letter: 'B',
 *          frequency: 0.01492
 *      }
 *  ]
 */
```

Note how we defined a custom type named "BarData," which is an array of objects (Object[]). We then list its properties and their types, to finish with an example of a bar chart data set. You can check the final code at this stage in the branch "step-1-documenting" of this chapter's repository (`http://bit.ly/pro-d3-docs-step-1`).

Creating these data types are an excellent opportunity to review our chart's API. In this case, we can observe that the current schema is tied to the first use we gave to this chart. However, a universal schema has generic keys like "category" instead of "letter" and "value" instead of "frequency." Some developers would go even further and start their coding by creating docs like this one, in a "readme-driven-development" way (`http://bit.ly/pro-d3-rdd`). This strategy is an exciting way of creating software that I encourage you to try at some point.

Generating the Documentation

In the previous section, we saw how to use the JSDoc syntax to describe the bar chart module and its functions. This documentation is helpful for contributors and maintainers working on the codebase. However, we also want to expose the API of the bar component to the users of the library.

To show that information, we employ documentation generators. These tools read our source code annotations to create documentation pages with them. There are many open source tools of this kind, and they can produce documentation in diverse formats like Markdown or HTML pages. In this section, we review some solutions and pick one to install, configure, and generate a custom documentation page.

Documentation Generators

Up to now, we have talked a lot about JSDoc. This project introduced documentation generation in the JavaScript world. Paradoxically, the default documentation created by JSDoc is neither beautiful nor usable. Many developers felt this pain and decided to create their JSDoc-compatible generators. In this section, we review a couple of these projects.

JSDoc to Markdown

The JSDoc to Markdown module (`http://bit.ly/pro-d3-jsdoc2md`) is a project that generates API documentation pages in Markdown format. It uses JSDoc annotations as a source, and we can choose to insert the generated documentation into our project's README.md file.

Installing and running this tool is simple, as it doesn't have any extra dependency. Most of the times, we only call the module and pass a source and output paths. When running this tool in our bar chart with "jsdoc2md -c jsdoc.conf.json src/charts/*.js", we got an output like the one in Listing 11-5.

Listing 11-5. JSDoc to Markdown output excerpt

```
## Bar
Bar Chart Reusable API component that renders a
simple and configurable bar chart.

**Requires**: <code>module:d3</code>
**Example**
```js
const barChart = bar();

barChart
    .height(500)
    .width(800);

d3Selection.select('.css-selector')
    .datum(dataset)
    .call(barChart);
```

* [Bar](#module_Bar)
```

* [exports(_selection, _data)](#exp_module_Bar--exports)
    * [.height([_x])](#module_Bar--exports.height) ⇒ <code>Number
    </code> \| <code>Module</code>
    * [.margin(_x)](#module_Bar--exports.margin) ⇒ <code>Object</code>
    \| <code>Module</code>
    * [.on()](#module_Bar--exports.on) ⇒ <code>Module</code>
    * [.width([_x])](#module_Bar--exports.width) ⇒ <code>Number</code>
    \| <code>Module</code>

<a name="exp_module_Bar--exports"></a>

exports(_selection, _data) ⬥
This function creates the chart using the selection as container

Kind: Exported function

Param	Type	Description
_selection	<code>D3Selection</code>	A d3 selection that represents the container(s) where the chart(s) will be rendered
_data	[<code>BarData</code>](#BarData)	The data to attach and generate the chart

<a name="module_Bar--exports.height"></a>

exports.height([_x]) ⇒ <code>Number</code> \| <code>Module</code>
Gets or Sets the height of the chart

Kind: static method of [<code>exports</code>](#exp_module_Bar--exports)
Returns: <code>Number</code> \| <code>Module</code> - Current height or
Chart module to chain calls
Access: public

Param	Type	Default	Description
[_x]	<code>Number</code>	<code>500</code>	Desired height for the chart

Note how we get an introduction of the bar chart module and the example we mentioned before. We also get a list of its public method descriptions. You can check the complete code at this point in the "step-2-documenting" branch of this chapter's repository (`http://bit.ly/pro-d3-docs-step-2`).

JSDoc to Markdown is an excellent fit to document a simple library that uses the README.md file as its documentation. This module also shines when used together with other static site generators.

Documentation.js

A popular project with more than 4000 GitHub stars, Documentation.js (`http://documentation.js.org/`) is a documentation generator that parses comments in JSDoc format. An alternative to the original JSDoc project (`https://github.com/jsdoc/jsdoc`), it provides a beautiful output, better ES2015+ support, and a modern internal implementation.

Documentation.js generates HTML, Markdown, or JSON outputs. It also supports several modern JavaScript modules like CommonJS, AMD, and ES2015+ modules. We can run it using Grunt or Gulp, but we prefer to use node scripts, as we see in the next section.

Other Options

We mentioned the previous projects because of their flexibility, but we have many options. Let's review some of them.

ESDoc

A project inspired by JSDoc, ESDoc (`https://esdoc.org/`) is a documentation generator focused on ES2015+ codebases. For the most part, it looks like a simplified JSDoc generator, and it has been used by projects like RxJS and ESDoc itself (`http://bit.ly/pro-d3-esdoc-docs`).

An exciting ESDoc feature is that it measures the documentation coverage. It even provides a GitHub badge to brag about it on your homepage. Also, we can include a link to our tests in the documentation of each module, so users can quickly check what the component can do.

Docusaurus

Created by the team at Facebook, Docusaurus (`http://bit.ly/pro-d3-docusaurus`) is a static site generator for open source projects. It bakes in some exciting features like versioning, search, internationalization, and a blog. Docusaurus uses Markdown as the input format to generate React (`https://reactjs.org/`) pages.

We could use Docusaurus with our JSDoc comments by extracting the documentation with JSDoc to Markdown. Then, we would use Docusaurus to incorporate the Markdown files into the documentation.

Docco

Jeremy Ashkenas – creator of CoffeeScript, Backbone.js, and Underscore.js – is the creator of Docco (`http://ashkenas.com/docco/`). This documentation generator takes a different approach. Docco creates HTML pages where it shows the documentation and code side by side.

Docco doesn't use JSDoc-type annotations. Instead, it uses inline comments to generate the documentation. This project can be useful when documenting a complicated piece of code or algorithm.

Generating Our Docs with Documentation.js

We have seen several projects that enable the creation of documentation from source code annotations. At this point, you might be wondering how this works in practice. That's why, in this section, we walk through the creation of a custom documentation page using Documentation.js.

Installation and Configuration

We install the npm package for Documentation.js by running "yarn add -D documentation". Then, we create a new npm script line in our package.json, calling it "docs:serve" and making it execute: "documentation serve src/charts/** -f html". In this command, we call Documentation.js with the argument "serve" to create a new dev server where we can see the documentation working. The "-f" option specifies the format, in this case, HTML. After running "yarn docs:serve" in a terminal window, we can navigate to "http://localhost:4001/" to see the documentation captured in Figure 11-1.

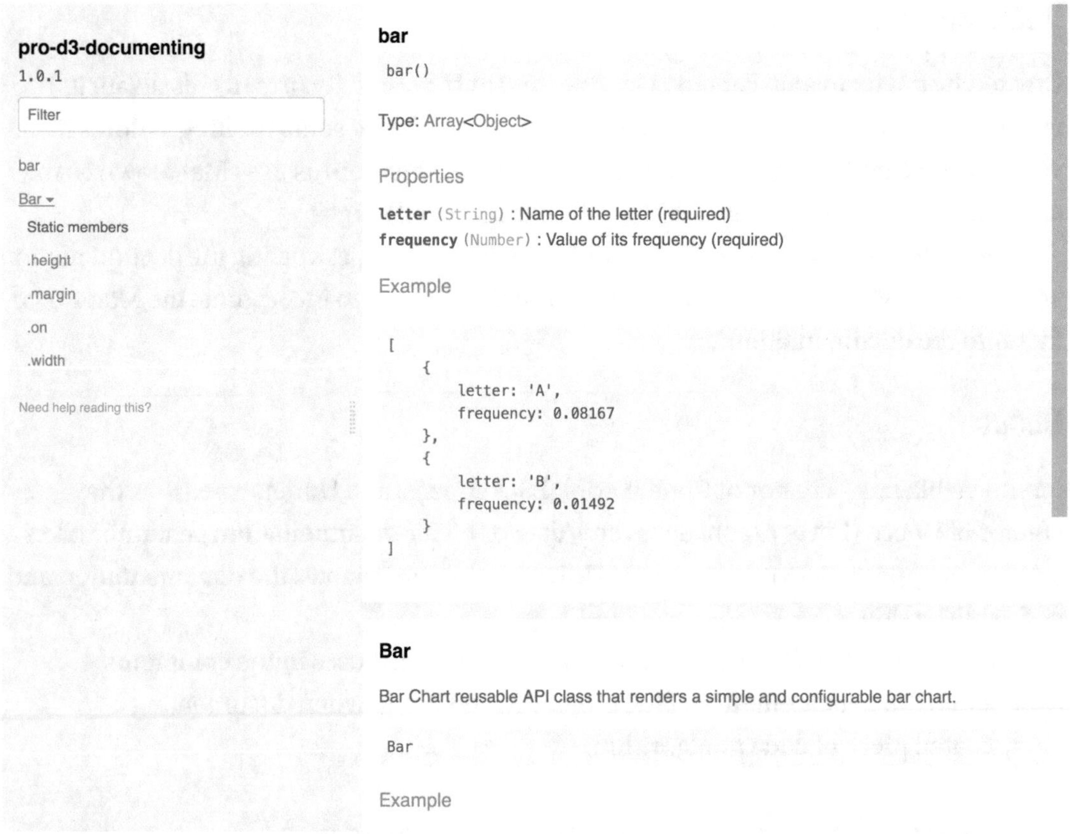

pro-d3-documenting

1.0.1

Filter

bar

Bar ▾

Static members

.height

.margin

.on

.width

Need help reading this?

bar

```
bar()
```

Type: Array<Object>

Properties

letter (String) : Name of the letter (required)
frequency (Number) : Value of its frequency (required)

Example

```
[
    {
        letter: 'A',
        frequency: 0.08167
    },
    {
        letter: 'B',
        frequency: 0.01492
    }
]
```

Bar

Bar Chart reusable API class that renders a simple and configurable bar chart.

```
Bar
```

Example

Figure 11-1. *Basic HTML page with Documentation.js*

Note that our generated documentation has the bar chart data schema and the API of the bar module. It also includes the current version of the library and a basic search. Figure 11-1 looks OK, but we want to include our Readme file as well. For it, we need to load a configuration object that in Documentation.js is a YAML file. We create it and fill it as in Listing 11-6.

Listing 11-6. documentation.yml configuration with grouped sections and Readme

```
toc:
  - name: Homepage
    file: README.md
  - name: Charts
    children:
```

```
      - Bar
  - name: Data Schemas
    children:
      - bar
```

Here we are also creating an extra level for "Charts" and "Data Schemas" so that we are ready to extend our library. Now, we need to tell Documentation.js that we want to use this configuration by using the "--config" option. This results in the script line of Listing 11-7.

Listing 11-7. Calling Documentation.js with a configuration file

```
"docs:serve": "documentation serve src/charts/** -f html --config
documentation.yml",
```

Running the previous command with Yarn in our terminal generates the documentation in Figure 11-2.

Figure 11-2. *Basic HTML page with Readme file*

Now we have some structured docs for our library. Although they are a bit bland, right? Let's fix it in the next subsection.

Customizing the Docs

We have seen how, using Documentation.js and a configuration object, we can achieve a nicely structured documentation page. However, we are still using the default styling and color schema, which is a bit boring. In the next paragraphs, we see how we can customize our docs by updating Documentation.js' default theme.

To begin, we copy the theme (`http://bit.ly/pro-d3-docjs-theme`) from the Documentation.js repository into the "src/docs/theme" folder of our project. We can also copy it from our own "node_modules" folder, searching for "documentation/src/default_theme".

In the next step, we use the "--theme" flag and point it to our copied theme, as shown in Listing 11-8.

Listing 11-8. Calling Documentation.js with a theme

```
"docs:serve": "documentation serve src/charts/** -f html --config
documentation.yml --theme src/docs/theme",
```

Running "yarn docs:serve" should give us the same result, but now we are ready to start customizing our theme. For this example, I navigated to `https://color.adobe.com/explore` and chose a color palette. Then, I updated "src/docs/theme/assets/style.css", creating some CSS variables with the chosen colors and applying them to different elements. After some minutes of work, I got the results we can see in Figure 11-3.

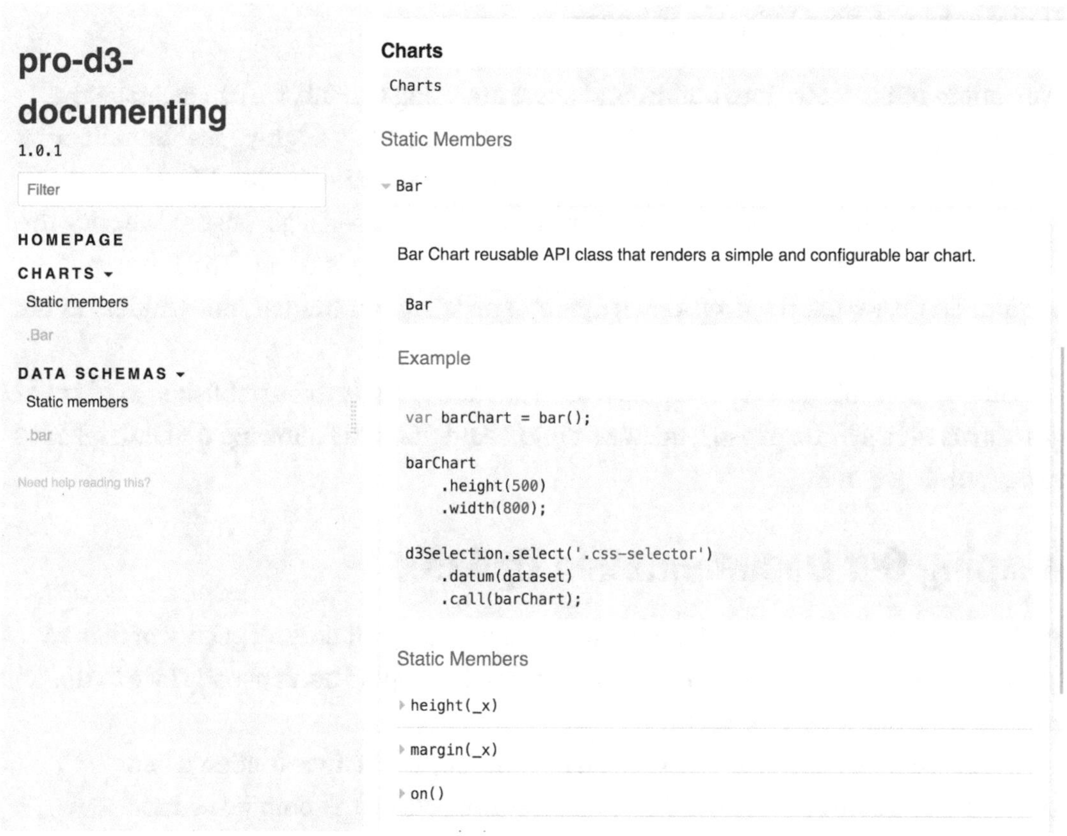

pro-d3-documenting

1.0.1

Filter

HOMEPAGE

CHARTS ▾

Static members

.Bar

DATA SCHEMAS ▾

Static members

.bar

Need help reading this?

Charts

Charts

Static Members

▾ Bar

Bar Chart reusable API class that renders a simple and configurable bar chart.

Bar

Example

```
var barChart = bar();

barChart
    .height(500)
    .width(800);

d3Selection.select('.css-selector')
    .datum(dataset)
    .call(barChart);
```

Static Members

▸ height(_x)

▸ margin(_x)

▸ on()

Figure 11-3. *Customized HTML page*

Not a huge change, but from here on, the only limit is our imagination! You can continue customizing the docs by downloading the code in the "step-3-documenting" branch of the repository (`http://bit.ly/pro-d3-docs-step-3`).

Publishing and Maintaining the Docs

We have seen how to annotate our source code with JSDoc comments. We also saw different projects to generate docs and how to use Documentation.js to create HTML documentation. However, it won't make sense to keep that documentation for ourselves: we should publish the docs in the Web! We also want to keep them up to date and extend them with more reference material.

For that, in this section, we are going to use GitHub Pages to publish our homepage. We also see how to maintain great docs by adding extra documents and enforcing comments using ESLint.

Publishing to GitHub Pages

We want to publish our docs online, and as we are using GitHub, we can leverage the GitHub Pages feature for it. We can do this either by targeting a "gh-pages" branch or by using our "/docs" folder in master. We'll go with the last option to simplify things.

Following the docs folder solution (`http://bit.ly/pro-d3-gh-pages`), we click the "settings" button on our GitHub repository. Then, we navigate to the "GitHub Pages" section. There, we use the drop-down menu to pick "master branch /docs folder" as our GitHub Pages source.

GitHub presents us with a link such as "Your site is ready to be published at `https://golodhros.github.io/pro-d3-documenting/`". And that's it! Following that link takes us to our published docs.

Keeping Our Documentation Updated

We have kept our documentation near the source code, so it doesn't get out of date so quickly. However, writing docs is something that developers don't usually love to do. How do we make it easy for them?

We can enforce our code standards using tooling and reduce friction when annotating the source code. For that, in this section, we learn about text editor extensions that ease the creation of JSDoc comments. We also see how to use ESLint to automate the requisite of comments on any new code.

Using Text Editor Extensions

A great way to influence developers to follow best practices is to make it easy for them to do so. In that line, text editor plugins help us fill in the JSDoc comments. See the following list of editors and extensions:

- **Sublime Text**: `http://bit.ly/pro-d3-sublime-jsdoc`

- **Visual Studio Code**: `http://bit.ly/pro-d3-vscode-jsdoc`

- **Atom**: `http://bit.ly/pro-d3-atom-jsdoc`

- **Vim**: `http://bit.ly/pro-d3-vim-jsdoc`

- **Emacs**: `http://bit.ly/pro-d3-emacs-jsdoc`

- **Webstorm (already integrated)**: `http://bit.ly/pro-d3-webstorm-jsdoc`

Most of them work by typing the JSDoc comment opening "/∗∗" and pressing the "Enter" key. This action generates a prefilled comment which we need to flesh out.

Enforcing Comments with ESLint

ESLint (https://eslint.org/) is a CLI linting utility for JavaScript. Created by one of my JavaScript heroes, Nicholas Zakas (https://humanwhocodes.com/), ESLint makes it easy to use rules and plugins to codify our code standards.

Installation

To install ESLint and the adaptors we need, let's jump into a console and type "yarn add -D eslint eslint-loader babel-eslint eslint-plugin-jsdoc". Then, we use the "eslint-loader" (http://bit.ly/pro-d3-eslint-loader) to create a loader in our Webpack parts file, as detailed in Listing 11-9.

Listing 11-9. The ESLint loader

```
exports.ESLintLoader = () => ({
    module: {
        rules: [
            {
                enforce: 'pre',
                test: /\.js$/,
                include: /src/,
                exclude: /node_modules/,
                use: ['eslint-loader'],
                options: {
                    failOnError: true
                }
            }
        ]
    }
});
```

We use the "enforce" option set to "pre" to make sure we run ESLint before babel, as we don't want to lint transpiled code. The "failOnError" option breaks the build when Webpack finds linting errors in our code. Lastly, we need to add "parts.ESLintLoader()" to our development pipeline within our webpack.config.js file as we can see in this file (`http://bit.ly/pro-d3-eslint-in-webpack`).

Configuring and Running ESLint

Now that we have ESLint in our development build, we need to configure it with the rules we want to check. The JSDoc-related rules are included in the "eslint-plugin-jsdoc" plugin (`http://bit.ly/pro-d3-eslint-jsdoc-plugin`). For this example, we selected some rules from the plugin's rule list:

- **jsdoc/require-jsdoc**: Requires the presence of comments in functions and classes

- **jsdoc/require-param**: Forces developers to specify all parameters

- **jsdoc/require-param-name**: Enforces a parameter name

- **jsdoc/require-param-description**: Requires a parameter description text

We can configure ESLint in the package.json or by creating a .eslintrc file. Let's go with the package.json way, as described in Listing 11-10.

Listing 11-10. ESLint configuration on package.json

```
"eslintConfig": {
  "parser": "babel-eslint",
  "parserOptions": {
    "ecmaVersion": 8,
    "sourceType": "module"
  },
  "plugins": [
    "jsdoc"
  ],
```

```
  "env": {
    "browser": true,
    "es6": true
  },
  "rules": {
    "jsdoc/require-jsdoc": ["error"],
    "jsdoc/require-param": ["error"],
    "jsdoc/require-param-name": ["error"],
    "jsdoc/require-param-description": ["error"]
  }
},
```

Here we are using the "babel-eslint" plugin (`http://bit.ly/pro-d3-babel-eslint`) as the parser and other options the ESLint team recommends in their configuration docs (`http://bit.ly/pro-d3-eslint-conf`). For the JSDoc rules, we declare that we want to throw errors when we miss JSDoc comments with properly described parameters.

Now, we need to run "yarn dev" to see our linting loader in action, pushing us to keep our code documented. You can check the whole code in the "step-4-documenting" branch of this chapter's repository (`http://bit.ly/pro-d3-docs-step-4`).

Extending Our Docs

We want to have great docs. There are many types of documents oriented to different target users: developers new to open source or the project, aspiring contributors, or seasoned open source wizards. Satisfying all while keeping an organization is challenging.

To solve this issue, we can organize our documents into four groups: Tutorials, How-to Guides, Topics, and Reference. Daniele Procida explained this approach in an article (`http://bit.ly/pro-d3-doc-types`). Let's see a definition of each of the groups.

Tutorials

A tutorial allows newcomers to get started with a project through a step-by-step guidance. It is essentially a lesson where we teach how to use our library. Chapter 7 of this book is a great example of a tutorial.

How-to Guides

In how-to guides, we show how to solve a problem with our library. Each step is a broad one, with less detail than a tutorial. It makes assumptions about the familiarity of the developer with the library so that we can achieve the intended goal faster. The section about ESLint in this chapter is a how-to guide, as we assume previous Webpack knowledge.

Topics

Topics or explanations give context to the architecture, design, and constraints of the project. They help users understand some of the decisions and why things were made the way they are. The explanation of the Reusable API from Chapter 4 is an excellent example of a topic article.

Reference

The description of a library is the goal of Reference documentation. They inform the user about the specific details of API methods, their inputs and returns, and when to use them. The best example of a reference is the module and data definitions generated with Documentation.js in this chapter.

Tutorials, How-to Guides, Topics, and Reference cover most of the surface area of a project and help to create diverse and welcoming communities. Most exceptional documentations contain pieces of all the previous types, and you can see a great example on Django's documentation (`http://bit.ly/pro-d3-django-docs`).

Summary

In this chapter, we have seen how to use source code annotations to generate an API reference for our library. We discovered how to publish our documentation and how to use ESLint to maintain our documentation coverage. Finally, we learned what kinds of documents comprehensive documentations include.

In the next and last chapter of this book, we will see how to use our D3.js charts along with the popular React.js library. We'll see the different strategies and render our bar chart within a React application.

CHAPTER 12

Using Your Library with React

React is a widespread and popular library for user interface development in JavaScript. At the same time, D3.js is the most successful library for creating visualizations for the browser. Their prevalence means that in many projects, we need to make them work together.

In this chapter, we will explore the use of D3.js charts within React applications. We will talk about React – the user interface library developed at Facebook. We will see how React renders views efficiently and how it relates to the D3.js way. We will explore different strategies to make React work along with D3.js. We will analyze these strategies, see examples of them, and discuss the benefits and drawbacks, as well as when to use each one. Finally, we will apply one of the strategies to the bar chart we created in previous chapters.

Because React and D3.js are opinionated libraries, both would fight for the control of the DOM elements on the page if used without care. So how can we make them work together? There are several ways, each optimized for different use cases. In this last chapter, we'll dive deeper into some of these strategies. However, we are going to start by analyzing the problem in more detail.

React, D3.js, and the DOM

Both React and D3.js were thought to, among other reasons, help developers deal with complex HTML and SVG markup. The former from a general user interface point of view, while the latter is more focused on handling vector graphics in the browser. To manage the DOM, React, and D3.js follow diverse approaches.

© Marcos Iglesias 2019
M. Iglesias, *Pro D3.js*, https://doi.org/10.1007/978-1-4842-5203-1_12

Back in the day, with jQuery, we accessed and manipulated DOM elements already rendered in our pages. Later, with Backbone.js and other MV* frameworks, we rendered views in response to changes in our data models. Now, with React.js, we became smarter about renders by using the virtual DOM, and with D3.js, we use data joins and the enter-update-exit pattern.

When talking about making React and D3.js work together, we need to understand a bit more about how they render the DOM. In this section, we discuss some fundamentals about React and D3.js. We also distinguish their way to deliver markup, establishing similarities between both libraries.

React

From the docs, React is a "JavaScript library for building user interfaces." Some characteristics differentiated this library from the rest on its inception:

- **Components first**: React was conceived to allow easy creation and composition of components to build large applications.

- **Declarative paradigm**: Using React, we list the components we want to show for each state and trigger re-renders. We never manipulate the DOM directly.

- **Multi-context**: With React, we create applications that we can render in the browser, a native mobile app, or even in virtual reality devices – all while following the same syntax.

The most celebrated feature of React is how it allows us to create and compose components. Using React, we arrange components by declaring their position within the JSX markup, and we render them. When we get new properties (or props, in the React jargon), we re-render the components to update the user interface.

Rendering and Reconciliation

React components use the virtual DOM to keep track of the rendered HTML. The virtual DOM retains a copy of the current markup in memory. When the state of the component changes, React compares the old state of the markup with the new markup and re-renders the component if necessary.

The "Reconciler" is the algorithm that compares the copy in the memory with the result of applying the new state. In version 16, the React team released a new architecture called Fiber, which includes a smarter and more efficient reconciler. You can learn about React reconciliation in this documentation article (`http://bit.ly/pro-d3-react-reconciliation`).

The "Renderer" is the logic that draws the user interface into the publishing target. We use different renderers depending on our target: Web, native, or virtual reality. These various renderers are similar to the way D3.js renders charts into different contexts such as HTML, SVG, or Canvas.

Dynamic Child Components

When we use React to render a list of items, we produce dynamic child components. In this scenario, we use unique keys to identify each descendant. These keys make re-rendering the component more efficient. They help React to figure out which child elements changed, so we don't re-render elements already present in the DOM.

With React, we use the unique keys, while when working with D3.js, the keys are the data attached to the DOM elements. Let's learn more about it in the next subsection.

D3.js

D3.js was conceived before the virtual DOM technique was popular. It has its own precursor libraries and inspiration, so it ended using widely different ways of managing the DOM elements. In this section, we talk about data joins (`http://bit.ly/pro-d3-joins`), so that we can establish connections with the way React works.

Data Joins

We can think of data joins as another DOM management approach. A data join is a set of DOM elements linked to data that helps us to transform the DOM.

To create a data join, we use the "d3-selection" module. We call the "selectAll" function with a CSS selector and execute the "data" method of the selection passing our data set. See our bar chart example in Listing 12-1.

Listing 12-1. A data join example from our bar chart

```
g.selectAll(".bar")
    .data(data)
    .enter()
      .append("rect")
```

```
.attr("class", "bar")
.attr("x", function(d) { return x(d.letter); })
.attr("y", function(d) { return y(d.frequency); })
.attr("width", x.bandwidth())
.attr("height", function(d) { return height - y(d.frequency); });
```

The data join happens in the first two lines of the previous code. Then, we use "enter" to declare what we do with the new data elements.

In Figure 12-1, we look at the relationship between a D3.js selection and the data. This diagram helps to illustrate how our data join creates the three groups: enter, update, and exit.

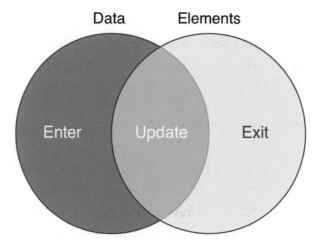

Figure 12-1. *Enter-update-exit pattern*

When we get new data, data points linked with existing elements gather into the update (central group) selection. The missing elements of the DOM produce the enter selection (left group). Finally, the remaining elements that don't have any data linked to them make the exit selection (right group). These are the elements we remove.

Once we create these three groups with the data join, we can operate over them independently. For that, we use the "enter," "update," and "exit" functions of the resulting selection. Having these three groups means that we can have different animations when adding, updating, or removing elements. It is worth mentioning that since "d3-selection" version 1.4, there is a new and convenient way of getting the same results by using "join." You can learn more about it in this Observable notebook (`http://bit.ly/pro-d3-join-notebook`).

In summary, when we create a data join, we are using a diff algorithm. Instead of comparing the DOM elements already rendered as we do with React, we compare their data. This data lives in the DOM, similarly as React keeps unique keys on child components. If we choose so, we can also pick the unique key in D3.js by using a "key function" in the "data" call (`http://bit.ly/pro-d3-selection-data`).

React and D3.js Working Together

We saw how React and D3.js help us in rendering user interfaces and data visualizations. D3.js draws chart elements in the DOM and transforms them depending on the data we give it. React also creates DOM elements, and it keeps track of them. When creating a React application that needs D3.js charts, we face the problem of who is to rule over the DOM. How can we make these two libraries work alongside when their strategies are opposed, and they were never meant to work together?

In this section, we go over four strategies to approach this dilemma. We review them starting with the approach closer to D3.js until we get to the more React-friendly strategy.

D3.js Within React

The first approach we cover gives control of the DOM to D3.js. I have called it "D3.js within React," and it is based on inserting the visualization code directly within a React class component.

In this strategy, we draw the root SVG element in our React component's render method. Next, within the "componentDidUpdate" lifecycle method, we create our visualization. We do it using D3.js and a reference to the root SVG node. In Listing 12-2 we can see an example.

Listing 12-2. D3.js within React example

```
import React from 'react';
import * as d3 from 'd3';

class Line extends React.Component {
    componentDidMount() {
        // D3 Code to create the chart
        // using this._rootNode as container
    }
```

```
shouldComponentUpdate() {
    // Prevents component re-rendering
    return false;
}

render() {
    return(
        <svg
            className="line-container"
            ref={this._setRef.bind(this)}
        />
    )
}
}
```

Note how we prevent the re-rendering of the component by hardcoding a false return from "shouldComponentUpdate".

Between the benefits of this approach, we can count its simplicity. It works fine for simple cases, at least until they grow into more complex data visualizations. This strategy is also the easiest when we already have an implemented visualization in D3.js, and we want to use it within a React application.

The drawbacks are that it is not idiomatic on React at all. It also mixes in the same file React code and a lot of D3.js code, creating a mixture that is not easily extendable and could become spaghetti code quickly.

However the drawbacks, this approach still has its uses. It is an excellent way to work if we are implementing a one of complex data visualization in D3.js. We could develop it until completion in vanilla JavaScript and D3.js and only then integrate it into a React component like the one in Listing 12-2.

React Faux DOM

The second approach involves a way of working similar to the previous, using D3.js to create the charts, but leaving the rendering part to React. React Faux DOM (http://bit. ly/pro-d3-faux-dom) is a data structure that acts like a DOM for D3.js, but that we can render with React.

As a fake DOM implementation, React Faux DOM supports most of the APIs that D3.js needs. Let's see an example in Listing 12-3.

Listing 12-3. React Faux DOM example

```
import React from 'react';
import * as d3 from 'd3';
import {withFauxDOM} from 'react-faux-dom';

class Line extends React.Component {
    componentDidMount() {
        // Creates a fake div and stores its virtual DOM inside the 'chart'
        prop
        const faux = this.props.connectFauxDOM('div', 'chart');

        // D3 Code to create the chart
        // using faux as container
        d3.select(faux)
            .append('svg')
        {...}

        this.props.animateFauxDOM(800);
    }

    render() {
        <div className="line-container">
          {this.props.chart}
        </div>
    }
}

export default withFauxDOM(Line);
```

Notice how we are doing most of the work on the "componentDidMount" lifecycle method of our React component. Moreover, we are using the high-order component (HOC) version so that we can benefit of "d3-transition" animations.

This strategy works great with stateless D3.js visualizations and static charts. Although it supports "d3-transition" when using the HOC, at some point, we could be forced to use a React animation library. This could be a benefit if you are already familiar with one. React Faux DOM allows us to use most of the D3.js APIs without problems, so it is great to integrate already built D3.js visualizations. Another positive feature is that we can do server-side rendering with our charts.

On the other side, using this approach, we could have issues integrating D3.js plugins. Because we are faking the DOM, and we add that on top of the virtual DOM, this method is, by definition, less performant. We are limited to medium size and complexity charts, although Thibaut Tiberghien offered some optimization tips in this article (`http://bit.ly/pro-d3-faux-optimized`).

I would recommend using this method when needing to integrate static or simple charts that we already built on D3.js. Another good use case is if we are looking for a hybrid approach using React animations while leaving the chart creation to D3.js.

Lifecycle Methods Wrapping

My favorite approach is this one. Using the "Lifecycle Methods Wrapping" strategy, we encapsulate our D3.js chart within a stateless module with a simple API. This module only exposes create, update, and destroy functions. Then, we create a React component which calls our chart's API within the "componentDidMount," "componentDidUpdate," and "componentWillUnmount" methods.

With this procedure, we create a clear boundary between our D3.js code and the React code. Credit for this method should go to Nicolas Hery for his article "Integrating D3.js visualizations in a React app" (`http://bit.ly/pro-d3-hery`). In Listing 12-4, we can see the React component.

Listing 12-4. Lifecycle Methods Wrapping example

```
import React from 'react';
import D3Line from './D3Line';

class Line extends React.Component {
    componentDidMount() {
        // D3 Code to create the chart
        this._chart = D3Line.create(
            this._rootNode,
            this.props.data,
            this.props.config
        );
    }
```

```
componentDidUpdate() {
    // D3 Code to update the chart
    D3Line.update(
        this._rootNode,
        this.props.data,
        this.props.config,
        this._chart
    );
}

componentWillUnmount() {
    D3Line.destroy(this._rootNode);
}

_setRef(componentNode) {
    this._rootNode = componentNode;
}

render() {
    <div
        className="line-container"
        ref={this._setRef.bind(this)}
    />
}
}
```

Note how we use a "ref" to keep track of the DOM element that contains our chart. We also hold the instance of our chart stored in the "_chart" instance variable, so we can update it when new props are provided. In Listing 12-5, we can see how the chart module would look like with pseudocode.

Listing 12-5. Lifecycle methods chart facade example

```
const D3Line = {};

D3Line.create = (el, data, configuration) => {
    // D3.js Code to create the chart
};
```

```
D3Line.update = (el, data, configuration, chart) => {
    // D3.js Code to update the chart
};

D3Line.destroy = () => {
    // Cleaning code here
};

export default D3Line;
```

Notice how basic this module is, exposing only three methods and encapsulating all the D3.js-related logic. We use this approach in Britecharts-React (`http://bit.ly/pro-d3-britecharts-react`), and we extend on it later in this chapter.

The benefit of this approach is a sharp distinction between the React and the D3.js code. This split helps with the maintenance of the system. Also, the chart module is super flexible, and we can use it to integrate our chart with frameworks like Angular, Vue, or any other. Lastly, using the "Lifecycle Methods Wrapping" strategy, it is easy to integrate any D3.js code.

For some developers, the use of an additional file could be seen as a drawback for this method. It is also clearly reliant on the D3.js way so that it is favored by D3.js developers more than by React developers.

I recommend this strategy most of the times, especially if you already have your D3.js charts built. It works great with the Reusable API pattern, as you see later in this chapter. I also suggest it whenever you plan to use the D3.js within React approach, as the overhead is minimal, and you increase maintainability.

D3 for the Math, React for the DOM

D3.js is a library formed by diverse modules that allow us to manage and transform data and to draw SVG elements in the DOM. With "D3 for the Math, React for the DOM" we leverage the D3.js modules that don't deal with the DOM to support React on creating data visualizations.

For example, we use D3.js to compute SVG paths, layout and format data, and generate scales. Then, we use React to draw these elements in the DOM and manage updates. Check Listing 12-6 to see a simple example of this approach.

Listing 12-6. D3.js for the Math, React for the DOM example

```
import React from 'react';
import * as d3 from 'd3';

class Line extends React.Component {
    drawLine() {
        let xScale = d3.scaleTime()
            .domain(d3.extent(
                this.props.data,
                ({date}) => date
            ))
            .rangeRound([0, this.props.width]);

        let yScale = d3.scaleLinear()
            .domain(d3.extent(
                this.props.data,
                ({value}) => value
            ))
            .rangeRound([this.props.height, 0]);

        let line = d3.line()
            .x((d) => xScale(d.date))
            .y((d) => yScale(d.value));

        return (
            <path
                className="line"
                d={line(this.props.data)}
            />
        );
    }

    render() {
        <svg
            className="line-container"
            width={this.props.width}
            height={this.props.height}
```

```
    >
        {this.drawLine()}
    </svg>
   }
}
```

Note how we create scales and lines as we did previously, although now we avoid the enter-update-exit pattern altogether. Using this strategy, we give the DOM rule to React.

The main benefit of this approach is the consistency with the React way of building components. We layout the elements of our visualization declaratively in our render function, and it feels terrific once we are done.

However, building charts with this approach implies a lot of work upfront. We need to reimplement some components that are shipped out of the box by D3.js. These are the axes, the zoom, dragging and dropping, and the brushes, among others. This strategy is also limited to SVG rendering, so we won't be able to switch into Canvas when the number of entries rises above the limit. Paradoxically, although this will be the preferred strategy for React developers, it is the one that requires more knowledge about the D3.js APIs.

Because of the previous drawbacks, I usually don't recommend creating a library from scratch using this strategy. Many interesting libraries take this approach, and you could fork and customize them for your needs. Libraries such as VictoryJS, Recharts, Nivo, or VX would save you tons of time when creating charts in this way. Nevertheless, you would need to learn their internals.

An exception to this advice is when you need to create a very niche charting library or when you plan to make a long-term investment on it. In these cases, the upfront work would be worth the effort.

Using Lifecycle Methods Wrapping with Our Library

We have seen how React and D3.js have mechanisms to help us deal with the DOM, allowing us to create user interfaces and visualizations. We saw four different strategies to integrate both libraries, some of them leaning on the D3.js side and some more close to the React way. In this book, we have covered the Reusable API extensively, and at this point, we have a bar chart in a production-ready state. How can we make it work within a React application?

In this section, we take the "Lifecycle Methods Wrapping" approach and use it to wrap our bar chart. We explore how to create our React chart component and a simple wrapper module for our reusable chart. We also see how to use the resulting React chart, so keep on reading!

Creating the Wrapper

The first thing we do is to create a minimal React component to wrap our bar chart. It is so simple that it only needs some modifications from the component shown in the previous section. Check Listing 12-7 for its code.

Listing 12-7. React component for our bar chart

```
import React from 'react';
import PropTypes from 'prop-types';
import D3Bar from './D3Bar';

export default class BarChart extends React.Component {

    static propTypes = {
        /**
         * Internally used, do not overwrite.
         */
        data: PropTypes.arrayOf(PropTypes.any),

        /**
         * Gets or Sets the height of the chart
         */
        height: PropTypes.number,

        /**
         * Gets or Sets the margin of the chart
         */
        margin: PropTypes.shape({
            top: PropTypes.number,
            bottom: PropTypes.number,
            left: PropTypes.number,
            right: PropTypes.number,
        }),
```

```
    /**
     * Gets or Sets the width of the chart
     */
    width: PropTypes.number,

    /**
     * Internally used, do not overwrite.
     *
     * @ignore
     */
    chart: PropTypes.object,
}

static defaultProps = {
    chart: D3Bar,
}

componentDidMount() {
    const { height, width, margin } = this.props;
    const configuration = { height, width, margin };

    this._chart = this.props.chart.create(
        this._rootNode,
        this.props.data,
        configuration
    );
}

componentDidUpdate() {
    const { height, width, margin } = this.props;
    const configuration = { height, width, margin };

    this.props.chart.update(
        this._rootNode,
        this.props.data,
        configuration,
        this._chart
    );
}
```

```
    componentWillUnmount() {
        this.props.chart.destroy(this._rootNode);
    }

    _setRef(componentNode) {
        this._rootNode = componentNode;
    }

    render() {
        return (
            <div
                className="bar-container"
                ref={this._setRef.bind(this)}
            />
        );
    }
}
```

Nothing too new here. We took Listing 12-4 and updated our chart name to "D3Bar".
We added "prop-types" to make sure we have all necessary properties. We also chose
to accept the configuration properties one by one. This means we need to build the
configuration object from our props before creating or updating our chart.

In the next piece of code, Listing 12-8, we implement the wrapper bar chart file. We
use the module we created in the previous chapters.

Listing 12-8. Bar chart wrapping module

```
import {select} from 'd3-selection';
import bar from './barChart';

const setChartProperty = (chart, configuration, key) => {
    if (configuration[key] || typeof configuration[key] === 'string') {
        chart[key](configuration[key]);
    }
};
```

```
const applyConfiguration = (chart, configuration) => {
    Object.keys(configuration)
        .forEach(setChartProperty.bind(null, chart, configuration));

    return chart;
};

const D3Bar = {};

D3Bar.create = (el, data, configuration = {}) => {
    const container = select(el);
    const chart = bar();

    container.datum(data).call(applyConfiguration(chart, configuration));

    return chart;
};

D3Bar.update = (el, data, configuration = {}, chart) => {
    const container = select(el);

    // Calls the chart with the container and dataset
    if (data) {
        container.datum(data).call(applyConfiguration(chart, configuration));
    } else {
        container.call(applyConfiguration(chart, configuration));
    }

    return chart;
};

D3Bar.destroy = () => {};

export default D3Bar;
```

See how both the create and update methods are pretty similar. One creates a chart instance, while the other takes the chart as an input parameter. Notice also how we use "applyConfiguration" and "setChartProperty" to apply the configuration to our chart. The first function takes the properties, and for each one, it calls "setChartProperty" passing the chart and the whole properties object. Within "setChartProperty," we configure the chart using bracket notation to call the accessor and passing its value as the argument.

Using Our Chart with React

To render our React chart, we need to create a new React application and pass the same data we used before to render our chart. In Listing 12-9 we can see an example of it.

Listing 12-9. Using the React-wrapped bar chart

```
import React from "react";
import ReactDOM from "react-dom";
import BarChart from "./BarChart";

const fixtureData = [
    {
        letter: "A",
        frequency: 0.08167
    },
    {
        letter: "B",
        frequency: 0.01492
    },
    ...
];

function App() {
    return (
        <div className="App">
            <BarChart
                data={fixtureData}
                width={800}
                height={400}
                margin={{
                  top: 50,
                  left: 50,
                  right: 50,
                  bottom: 50
                }}
            />
```

```
        </div>
    );
}
```

```
const rootElement = document.getElementById("root");
ReactDOM.render(<App />, rootElement);
```

Using our bar component is when we experience React's delightful developer experience and declarative syntax. You can see these files in this chapter's source code or play with them in this CodeSandbox example (`http://bit.ly/pro-d3-lifecycle-sandbox`).

Take into account that this is not a production-ready component. To become one, it would need tests for the React component and the D3.js chart wrapper. We should also need to add some defensive code to validate the configurations. You can see these and more improvements in the Britecharts-React (`http://bit.ly/pro-d3-britecharts-react-bar`) version of this code.

Summary

In this chapter, we learned how the most successful data visualization library and the most popular user interface library manage the DOM. We have discussed how to use both at the same time. We learned the different strategies we can follow, how do they look in code, their benefits, drawbacks, and when to use each one.

We also discovered how we could apply one of the strategies to the reusable chart we created in previous chapters. Finally, we saw how we could wrap our D3.js code and use it within React applications.

With this chapter, we arrived at the end of this book. In it, you have learned to transform your D3.js charts into professional, well-tested, and maintainable code.

Now go out there and create your chart library! Enjoy a great developer experience and publish it so that the community can delight in your work and help you make it awesome.

Moving forward, you can keep up with myself (`https://twitter.com/golodhros/`) and Britecharts (`https://twitter.com/britecharts/`) on Twitter. I also recommend you join the D3.js community in our Slack workspace (`http://bit.ly/pro-d3-slack`). There you can connect with other D3.js specialists, get support, and meet great people.

Thanks for reading!

Index

A

API testing
  height accessor
    code, 148
    test, 147, 148
  margin accessor
    code coverage, 150, 151
    test, 149, 150
Arrow functions, 7

B

Babel
  browsers, 172
  configuration, 173
  definition, 172
  Webpack, 173, 174
  webpack-merge, 174
babelLoader, 160, 165
Bar chart
  adding SVG element, 14
  axes, 17
  data loading, 16, 17
  margin convention, 15
  scales, 15
  use SVG rectangles, 18–21
Britecharts, 42
  adding tooltip, 101, 102
  bar chart, 79
  branch creation, 117, 118

create legend, 103–105
creating chart
  configuring, 98–100
  setting up container, data set,
    chart, 96, 98
  throttling a function, 100, 101
customizing styles
  color palette, 110, 111
  Google fonts, 112, 113
data visualization
  brush chart, 88
  legend, 90
  mini-tooltip, 89, 90
  tooltip, 89
demos, 116, 117
donut chart, 81, 82
downloading, 96
filtering data, brush
  configuring, 107, 108
  creating, 105
  generating, 106, 107
  wiring event, 108–110
formatting, 93, 94
grouped bar charts, 79, 80
library documentation, 116, 117
modification
  API description, 121
  bar chart animationDuration
    accessor, 120–122
  failing test, 118, 119

M. Iglesias, *Pro D3.js*, https://doi.org/10.1007/978-1-4842-5203-1

W, X

Y, Z

Printed in the United States
By Bookmasters